TEENAGE KiCKS

a true story of dark streets to bright new beginnings

SiAN YOUNG

Teenage Kicks
a true story of dark streets to bright new beginnings

First published in 2012 by
Ecademy Press
48 St Vincent Drive,
St Albans, Herts, AL1 5SJ
info@ecademy-press.com
www.ecademy-press.com

Printed and bound by Lightning Source in the UK and USA
Designed by Neil Coe

Printed on acid-free paper from managed forests. This book is printed
on demand, so no copies will be remaindered or pulped.

ISBN 978-1-907722-95-0

This book is available online and all good bookstores.

ACKNOWLEDGMENTS

I dedicate this book firstly to my wonderful son, for he is a true gift from the gods.

I next send my deepest love to Jennifer who taught me how to be a woman and showed me the love of a mother. May she rest in peace.

I thank also all the people who have touched my life and have caused me to learn. I thank the people who put up with me while I was in a desperate state and to those who helped me on my healing journey. Thank you to all the strong women I know, without them I would be lost. I wish nothing but blessings be bestowed upon you and the people you love.

To my nan and granddad for being the one constant connection with my family. I thank my mother for giving me life, I am very thankful that we have such a good loving relationship now.

A special mention to Poppy who has been an unwavering friend in my life and has always let me know that I can achieve anything I desire and that anything is possible.

Thank you, Paula Hogg, for your continued belief in me and my power and your homeopathic treatments. You always know what I need and you are always right.

Thank you to the Samaritans who are always there when I call and to the free local counselling agencies who helped hold my hand through some deep healing.

I thank Kelis Groghty for the Reiki healing and guidance she gave me as this was the key to the beginning of my healing process. I thank Yasmeen for pushing me to bring this book into reality and supporting its growth.

OVERViEW

My book *Teenage Kicks* contains stories about parts of my life so far – not all as this would take many books. I have called it *Teenage Kicks* as it is a book containing stories of things I got up to when I was a young homeless girl aged 15 on the streets of Scotland. What I have tried to do in this book is to take you back with me to each stage I have lived and grown, by using colourful Scottish language along with powerful descriptions of sights, sounds and smells.

When reading this book you will experience my tongue-in-cheek sense of humour, along with the hope, joy and grains of love that have made it possible for me to survive such an existence. I will show you the real subculture of the drug, party and street culture that exists in Fife and Edinburgh from a homeless girl/ woman's point of view. I have also made it possible for you to step back and see all the players on the stage. To see how feeders (feeders are those that lure vulnerable people into their web with a mind to abuse them for financial gain) take a hold of vulnerable children and young people then abuse them.

I hope this book will give you a valuable insight into drug street culture, self-harm and self-abuse, how a person can get lost and how you can come to a stage in your life where your worth is not realised, even by yourself. I want to help young people who are continually abused and abusing themselves. There is a contact list of agencies that are safe and supportive to these needs at the back of the book. We are all special. These stories do not run in a chronological order, they are individual stories written from the perspective and memories of a teenage girl. That teenage girl who was, and of course still is, me. I feel that readers will be able to relate to one, if not more, of the situations I have lived through. I hope they will gain some strength in the knowledge from my experiences, as I know I have.

"To know you are not alone and that you *can* and *will* make positive changes to your life no matter how bad your life may be, so take heart, you can and will heal yourself, it is up to you."

Me after homelessness

CONTENTS

CHAPTER 1

Home Sweet Home

I would like to start this book by sharing with you some of the names and sweet messages I grew up with as a young developing woman; this I hope will help you understand some of the choices I have made in my life. First to share with you the endearing names given to me by my stepfather George (who married my mother when I was four years old) such as Bitch, Slut, Crab, Slag, Lying Bastard – all the kind of names to help me grow up feeling loved and respected as a young woman. Some other lovely comments he would say (by saying 'lovely' I am sure you can hear my sarcasm): "No one would want to be your friend, bitch, unless they wanted something from you; who you going to fuck tonight, slag?" The sort of comments that make it impossible (no matter how hard you try) to go into a group of young teenagers and feel as though you really belong and that they are really your friends and not just there to get what they want from you. I was about 12 when these comments started, as far as I can remember. The more the years passed, the more my brain struggled to find myself and respect myself; I started to act like a fucked up teenager.

I will now share with you some of the memories of growing up.

"Katie," says George.
"Yes."
"You have a choice: you can come fishing with me at 5:30 this morning or you can stay in bed," he responds.
To me this means getting up at 5:30 on a weekend and sitting freezing and damp next to a river with your rod out.
The bonus however is fresh chicken, salad, Coca-Cola and all sorts of goodies or… "If you don't that's fine! But what you may eat out of the fridge is this Edam and bread," he continues.

Humm! Let me see? I ponder: on one hand bread and cheese and on the other chicken, salad, cola, crisps and cakes?

"I am coming fishing," I shout downstairs to him.

I cannot remember much about these fishing trips, probably because they were too early in the morning for my brain to be fully operational, but for sure my taste buds were. It really depends on how hungry or how tired I am, whether or not I choose to go.

"Katie!" George shouts to me. "You want to come fishing tomorrow?"

"No thank you! I am tired and need some sleep; it has been a hard week at school!"

"Fuck off you lazy bitch, school isn't hard work!" he shouts at me.

Just the kind of reply he would give, as if he remembers school anyway – he is a dorky relic.

"You have to do the ironing pile and I want you to have finished it before we get back, oh and the dishes as well. OK? Or you will be grounded for the rest of the weekend."

I come downstairs and look at the ironing pile nearly the size of me, full of his navy eights (this is what they call his uniform, it is hard to iron and you have to iron the creases right in the centre of the trousers; they are fireproofed so they are heavy and a bugger to iron). He has the cheek to call me lazy. He is the lazy one, off out fishing leaving me with the chores. Bang goes the weekend, it seems if I denny get this done, I will kiss goodbye seeing any of my friends.

Night passes and I hear them leave, taking their fresh chicken picnic with them. Sometimes you just gotta eat the cheese and bread and rest. I am chilling listening to music in my room when I suddenly remember I haven't done my chores, shit! I run downstairs and flash up the iron and run the dish water, better get into it.

Ahh! Job well done, my freedom has been bought for the rest of the weekend. As I relax I realise that I am thirsty; I look in the fridge, there are about 24 mini cans of cola and soft blue cheeses, salami and a punnet of peaches.

I know not to bother eating any soft blue cheeses or salami but surely I can have a peach and a wee can of coke after all that hard work. It's like a Chinese laundry in here. I succumb and take the coke and peach and make my way up to my room. I am lying on my bed chilling again, eating such a juicy peach followed by the fizzy thirst-quenching drink of a cool cola; life is bliss.

"We are back, have you done your chores?" George is obviously keen to know.
"Yes," I shout down the stairs. I can see out my bedroom window my mother unpacking the car, my brother who is four years younger than me asleep on the back seat.
I come downstairs to show off my lovely work in the Chinese laundry-cum-sweatshop.
"Well, you can go out tonight," says George.
As he is unpacking the leftovers of the picnic I ask, "Did you catch anything?"
"No," he replies as he opens the fridge to put some of the leftovers in; then, "You thieving fucking bitch!" he is yelling

right in my face.

"What?" I ask, confused.

"You have been fucking drinking my cokes, there's one missing, I counted them before I went out."

"I was thirsty," I say apologetically.

"You could have drunk water, you thieving bitch."

"Fuck you, I have just done all your eights and the rest of the ironing and the dishes and you begrudge me a mini can of coke."

"What did you fucking say?" He is looking at me like he is about to burst. I start to run out the kitchen past no-man's-land, turn left and bolt up the stairs trying to reach the relative safety of my room.

"Come back bitch," shouts George as he starts to take chase. He quickly loses his breath at the bottom of the stairs, also known as no-man's-land.

"You're fucking crazy, all I done was eat and drink," I shout from my room.

Just then the door opens and my mother walks in. "Can't I leave you two alone for five minutes without trouble starting?" she asks. Mum is the regular peacekeeper. "What's going on?" she asks George.

"Fucking bitch stole my coke, she is always stealing my stuff," he tells her.

"Calm down George, I will go and talk to her," she responds.

The door to my room opens and my mum's head is peeking around the door. "What has been happening?" asks Mum.

"That crazy fucker is chasing me because I ate one of his precious peaches and drank a coke after I have ironed all his work clothes," I tell her.

"I will have less of that language, girl, there is no need for that, he is just upset and tired. Just walk away and ignore him," she says.

"That's easy for you to say but he doesn't allow me to and anyway I am the child, I shouldn't have to walk away, he should sort his head out."

It is a couple of weeks later and I am off to meet some friends, my make-up is on and my hair is done just right and if I do say so myself, I am looking good. All I have to do now is get past George without any painfully embarrassing and degrading game play.

"Katie!" Where are you going?" asks George.

I am in no-man's-land at the bottom of the stairs, the living room to my right, the kitchen to the left, in front of me is the bright light shining through the slated window which represents freedom, also known as the front door.

"I'm just going to hang out in Rothsy," I reply.

"Wait there, I want to see you," he says.

I see him coming from the left, he is carrying something in his hands, I am not quite sure what it is.

"Let me look at you," he says.

I turn around to face him.

"Let me look at you," he says again with his hands now hidden behind his back. "What you all dolled up for, you tart, going to get some boys?" he continues. I am thinking he must have one sick mind to be able to come up with all these perceptions of my behaviour. I am just a teenager going to hang out with my mates.

CHAPTER 1

"No, just …"

My words are broken off; the nutter is launching at me, he has come in with such speed I can't see what is going on. Then, as quick as he came, he is standing back in his start position spraying a stream of sticky liquid at me, up and down, it is getting in my face, my mouth, my eyes and as it does I can taste the rancid chemicals of the liquid as it hits my lips making me gag. I don't know what else he has done but my head feels restricted and it is dripping with something thick and cold. He has stopped now and is standing back admiring his work. As the horror subsides I reach for my head to feel what is restricting me realising that he has put a pair of pants on my head and smashed an egg in them and I am covered with washing-up liquid.

"Where you are going looking like that, Katie?" he mocks with a big grin, proud of his latest attempt to crush my spirit.
"Fuck you, asshole!!" I yell.
"Your language is terrible, did the washing-up liquid not do a good enough job? I could always wash your filthy mouth out with a bar of soap," says George.

I take his threat seriously as he has done this before. A shiver runs down my spine as I remember the day I was held in a deadlock with him holding my nose shouting, "Chew on that you fucking filthy bitch." I could no longer keep my mouth closed and when I opened it so I could to get a breath he had rammed the bar of soap in my mouth hitting it off my teeth. As he was shoving it in shavings started to go down my throat and my mouth had begun to foam. I will never forget the taste of soap. He is the inspiration for my vocabulary.

I am fed up with living with the constant fear and acts of humiliation. The only time I feel respected and safe from attack is when my sister, brother, mother and I are home alone and the bastard is at sea. I can remember going to the social work department and sitting in the waiting room. A lady came to see me and all I could say was, "I am not happy, please help me." The social worker came round to my house to help our family work out our differences and try to get along. I also remember just wanting someone to talk to. George told me what went on inside the house was our family's business, not anybody else's. I told him, "You have my mum to speak to, I have no one, it's not fair." He had put on an angelic face and won them over and soon all was back to normal. The happy days were when I was told George was off to sea for a six-month tour of duty. This time went fast. I felt human again instead of a slimy enema. My mother is a wonderful woman and I don't know how she puts up with him. I suppose to live on your own with three children and no money is a good enough reason to be scared to change the situation. I often wondered if she noticed the change in herself when he came home; it was like a veil was pulled over her shining light.

I am lying on my bed in my room. It is late when suddenly I smell the familiar smell that tightens all my veins and causes me a straight headache: smoke. Smoke can only mean that George is back from sea and will start exerting his control very soon.

I hate him, he makes me shrink and I start to stress as I see his face in my mind's eye. His round, fat, ball-like face with a bad barnet of wavy dark brown hair cut into a bowl cut, his beard that extenuates his ball face and the disgusting noise as he chews it in the corner of his mouth when he thinks what he was doing was funny. He is only a short man but with a big stomach who wears bad clothes – horrible-fitting jeans and T-shirts with collars.

I do not sleep well as I am worried for what the next day may bring. In the morning I am woken up by another familiar sound: George hacking up phlegm in the toilet which is right next to my room.

"Good morning Katie, are you going to join us? I have already gone shopping, come downstairs and see," George asks as he pokes his head around the door. "Oh, and are you thinking of cleaning your room at any point in the near future as it fucking stinks?"

"Good morning." I squeeze the comment out, wondering if he realises I am tired because I have been stressing all night about seeing him.

"Come on Katie, come downstairs," he says again.

'Oh, what now? He is back, the big adolescent with power over me', I think to myself.

"Look, I have been to the shops and I will tell you what you are allowed and what you are not; now this stuff is mine and your mother's," he says, pointing to a drawer in the fridge with nice deli food in it, "and this is you kids' food." He points to the other drawer with a lump of Edam and cheddar. What a thing to wake up to! I mean it's bad enough, he is freaky about his food but to then wake me up to show me what I can't have is sadistic. George is home!

"I want to spend some time with you and Jack tonight so you will both stay in, OK?" George says, sounding as if we had a choice.

'What fun' I think as me and my brother are sitting in the brightly-lit living room, it is quite a long room, rectangle in shape. You enter the room, there is a chair opposite the door and behind it a big mahogany cabinet, then right around the door is another chair and the light is situated over these chairs. Then as you look further up the room you come to the sofa against one wall and another cabinet against the opposite one and the TV in the far corner tucked away facing the sofa. On the sofa lies King Tubby (George). In between him and the cabinet is the glass-topped coffee table on which he is lining up his Maltesers along the rim where the glass meets the wood. One by one he is eating them and watching TV. My brother and I are held prisoners just watching him.

"Why are we here, we are just watching you watch TV?" I ask.
"Spending time together," replies George.
"Can Jack and I have Maltesers then, please?" I ask.
"Yeah... when you have some money you can buy some," he says back.
He is so childish – has he never learnt to share? Anyway he has a multipack in the cabinet opposite him. Me and my brother wait there in silence looking at each other and then at King Tubby and then the TV. Ah! How we love special family time with George! Then he turns around and throws a Malteser at us; if we don't catch it, we need to find it and eat it wherever it is on the floor or covered in fluff, or we don't get one. He treats us like dogs.
"You can always have toast," suggests George.
Story of my life! Fuck that, I will wait till night time.

I have been sent to bed now but I will not sleep; I will wait till Mum and George have gone to bed and all is silent.

The time has come to go on my mission! Slowly I open my door and turn around to the right but I have to be careful, there is a creaky floorboard right outside my room, so as light as a fairy I have to skip over it to the banister. I follow the banister to the end of the landing and to the top of the stairs. Mum and George's room is right next to me and I am sweating at the thought of him coming out, terrified I will fall down the stairs with the fright.

I let this thought pass and concentrate on the mission; I have noted where all the creaky stairs are so I need to concentrate. I make my way down the stairs slowly, carefully, there's no way I want to wake King Tubby.

I am shallow breathing, I have now reached no-man's-land, I turn left but I will have to jump on to the wooden divider in the door frame as the floor creaks badly here. I am balanced on the wooden divide and am trying to open the door without any noise. Slowly I pull down on the handle till the door opens. Next to the door is the fridge and its sound breaks the silence; I must be quick now! I carefully and precisely swing my body around to the other side of the door and silently shut it, sealing the fridge noise out to the sleeper upstairs. I am in but this is only half the mission.

I am standing with my back against the door taking a breath; across from me I see the microwave is shining its light – time 12:30 a.m. Slowly, quietly and carefully I open the fridge and leave it open to provide extra light as the kitchen light has a familiar buzzing noise when it is turned on. I start to slide out the forbidden drawer. Aahh! The soft cheeses and delicate pâtés! I reach on top of the fridge for the cracker box and carefully place it on to the side next to the cooker. I remove the crackers from the bottom layer of the box then proceed to make up my delicious nibbles of all the forbidden food. I reach across the back of the counter and tear some kitchen roll and line them up so that I can wrap up each nibble carefully.

I admire my work and then set about clearing all evidence of my arrival. I then turn over the waistband of my pyjamas and place my bootie inside the turn-up. I pour a glass of milk, this will be my cover if I am caught. OK, now back to base (base being my bedroom). I listen at the door, pushing my ear right against it trying desperately to hear any tell-tale sounds of George. The sound of the fridge is right next to me and I have to wait until the lull in its cycle so I can listen properly.

I am sure he is there behind the door waiting to pounce on me; I'm sure I can hear him breathing. The clock shines 1:00 a.m. I must get to base! But what if he is behind the door? The stress is hurting my head, the fear, and the tiredness. I have school tomorrow and must get to bed. "Fuck it, I will just open this door, if he is there or not I don't care, I must go now!" I say to myself. But what if he is there? I can't bear it so I slide down behind the door and sit on the floor in fear for what seems like hours, scared and going quietly mad. The fridge has a break in its cycle; I listen intently at the door and I slowly pull down the handle and open the door. The relief hits all of my muscles and bones which have been stiff with fear for so long. I am again in no-man's-land, taking the same carefully charted route back to base, and as I slowly open my door the smell of victory is sweet and so too is the scent of my booty.

I climb back into my bed and plump up the pillows, getting comfy now; I line up my booty along my left leg, which one first? One by one I open my stashed food parcels and as I put each one in turn slowly into my mouth, savouring each morsel, it becomes apparent to me how comforting food can be. A sweet warming sensation comes over my body and I feel pleased as the tastes sink into my tongue; the stress that was involved getting them slowly and calmly leaves my body until only the delicious tastes are left in my mouth.

I break my trance but for only a second to hide my kitchen towel under my bed for disposal in the morning, then as quick as I had left it I was entranced again. I snuggle down under the covers taking this feeling with me and then sleep comes, a deep and satisfying sleep.

A few weeks have passed and I am happy to hear George is going back to sea soon. I have organised to meet some friends and am looking good again (even if I do say so myself). Of course, as usual George has his own agenda; today he is trying to look cool.

"Is that what you are wearing?" asks George.

"Yes," I say, waiting for it.

"Look at this," George says to my brother, then he grabs me and hauls me along the landing towards the toilet. I don't know what is coming next and I start to fight to set myself free, trying to wedge my hands and legs in the bathroom door so he can't get me in.

"Fuck off, what are you doing?" I am protesting.

"You will see," says George who then gives me a powerful push and all I can see is the toilet coming closer. I try to fight and put my hands out to stop my head from getting any closer. He wins. He pulls my arms by my side and holds them, forcing me to stay powerless to his game. I close my eyes as I feel the cold water at the bottom of the toilet on my head. He is ramming my head down the toilet then he flushes the chain and the water begins to rise over my head. He pulls me out and laughs at me. I am standing there with my hair limp with toilet water around my face, my make-up all run, with one earring in the toilet. I feel distraught and confused.

"What you do that for, you sicko?" I ask.

"You had too much hairspray on your fringe so I thought I would help you get it off," laughs George.

"You are sick in the head," I say to him with disgust.

George looks to my brother for approval of his sick game, looking for him to join in on the fun! He finds none. My brother, looking ashamed of him, turns and walks away.

CHAPTER 2

is the Grass Really Greener?

"You will see how it is to live in someone else's house then maybe you will appreciate what you have here!"

These are the words I hear as my mum is packing my bag. She is packing me away to stay with this crazy alcoholic in Dysart; this woman has had her children staying at my house as my mum is a community carer.

I go and get the bus to Dysart, very excited to see what this adventure teaches me; anyway I am glad to get a break from George as he is a nippy bastard.

I arrive at the bus stop in Dysart after a gruelling two-and-a-half hours on the boneshaking express. I climb off the bus; Karen is there to meet me.

As I look around, I notice two old ladies walking along the road with blue pencilled-on eyebrows. This scares me, and I make my mind up there and then never to pluck my eyebrows.

"Hi Katie, how's it going?" Karen asks.

"Well you know, not bad, what's happening in good old Dysart today?" I reply.

"My grandmother died yesterday so Mum's sorting her flowers; here, let me give you a wee tour de Dysart. On the left we have the disused gas works; if you strike a match and throw it at it maybe we could have some good fireworks the night. On the right we have Palace de Dysart where me, my sisters and my ma live. Come in Katie, I'll show you where to put your bags."

As I walk in the house and up the stairs with the brown spiral-pattern carpet, I notice a strong smell of Shake n' Vac. I continue along the hall when Sharon comes out of a door on my left.

"Hi Katie, why don't you put your bag in here just now, this is where you will be sleeping."

I go into the room which is very tidy. There is a lot of pattern in the carpet and the bed sheets and the wallpaper is a carousel of swirls.

It is cold in here and the windows are mouldy. They are rotting and look and feel like they hold no heat.

"Here," says Karen, "this is your bed for your stay." She motions towards a bed on the right of an old dresser.

"Thanks."

"Who's that, girls? Is that Katie here?" Geraldine shouts from the living room.

"Yes Mum," Karen replies back. "Come on, we better go and see her before she goes off on one!"

I notice that the girls are tense. I follow them along the flowery-wallpapered hall past another two doors, one on the right and one on the left; this is the back room I think, then through the door at the end of the hall into the living room.

"Come in girls, let me meet Katie. Hello my dear, how was your journey?" Geraldine asks me.

"The bus was a total boneshaker but I am glad to get here. How are you?" I say.

"Well, I have been having a hard time, my mother died yesterday; hey girls what do you think?" Geraldine says, as she is showing us a large bunch of red roses.

"They're beautiful," I say.

"Yeah! Nan will be really pleased," Jessie says.

Jessie is one of the four sisters that live here; they also have a wee sister who is only six months old, called Carrie.

"So here," says Geraldine, "let's all kiss the roses before I take them down to the funeral parlour tomorrow." We all kiss the roses.

The next day Geraldine is away to the funeral; Jessie, Sharon and Carrie go with her.
Karen and I go to this old man's house that Karen says she looks after. We arrive at his house just across the square at the back of Geraldine's house.
"James, it's me," Karen shouts through the letter box. He will not answer if he thinks it's the social worker or young boys, she tells me.

"Come on James, it's me, open the fucking door, it's Karen come to cash your giro for ya."
We hear this kinda grunting and hoarse shouting.
"All right, keep your hair on, I'm coming lass I didny hear ye!" shouts James as he walks to the door.
"You better hold ye breath, it fucking stinks in there, oh and don't touch the walls, OK?" Karen warns me.
When the door opens the smell of shit and old sweat hits me right at the back of my nostrils causing me to gag.
"Who the fuck is that?" James asks, pointing to me.
"Ah she's all right. Keep your head on old man. She's a mate and she's staying with me," says Karen.

We go in. Karen was right to tell me not to touch anything; there is shit smeared along the walls of the hall and the carpet is also thick with it and years of ground-in dirt. On my right is a bedroom carrying on the theme of spiral wallpaper, the green dirty curtains are closed but some light is still making it through as they sway in the breeze coming in through the hole in the window.

On my left I can see the kitchen with maggots and flies in the sink and all around there are dirty dishes piled so high that they nearly topple over. There are open cans everywhere you look. The toilet which is next door to the kitchen is yellow with pee. Piles of shit are rotting around the bottom of it and there are flies hovering around it, even the handles have dried crusty shit on them. I am trying not to add to the disaster by being sick. I know if I start I won't stop.

We enter his living room at the end of the hall.
"He's a smelly shit, eh Katie?" says Karen.
"Yeah," I whisper.
"It's all right, he is as deaf as a post, you need to shout for him to hear you, the old man used to be a coal miner that's why he has them lumps on his head."
"What's that?" says James at the volume of someone who is stone-deaf and has problems hearing their own voice.
"He won't get a hearing aid, don't like nobody, he's a grumpy bastard," says Karen as she turns to me.
"What's that, hen?"James says.
"I was just asking if you needed any money put in the meter, James," Karen says as she turns to face him.
"Yes please doll."

"What do you need from the shop?"
"I want a couple o' they condensed milk cans, you ken what I mean hen, tea bags and fags, you know, tobacco like, you know the one I have," James says.

"Hey, come here Katie, look." Karen is showing me just how to work an electricity meter with plastic fifty pence pieces, you know, the ones you get from a toy till. She gets me to come around James's chair into a thin cupboard where the meter is, she puts them in the slot and turns the dial and hey presto – electricity! She then puts the fifty pence in her pocket. I'm learning a lot already in only one day on my tour de Dysart.

"What are you doing behind there, lassie? Come here." James is calling me to sit down on the chair in front of him.

"Where you from then?"

"I am from Rothsy," I say.

"What, girl? You need to speak up, I can't hear you."

I am trying not to gag as I see him in front of me. He is a round-faced man with blotches on his skin; his shoulders all hunched over his skin, looks like it used to fit his body but now was overgrown. I see he has long fingernails stained with years of tobacco smoke; as I look closer I see they have lumps of shit under them. He wipes his hand across his snotty nose and the bogies are streaming down from his nose to his hands as he promptly wipes them on his already bogie-ridden top. His trousers are solid with shit and dirt. He is sitting across from me with his flies broken and his dirty limp penis is hanging in full view. I am finding it extremely hard to hear what he is saying as I am trying not to be sick.

"I come from Rothsy," I shout, trying not to take in any air when I open my mouth. Then I have to leave the room.

I go into the bedroom. The hole in the window is the only source of fresh air where the neighbourhood boys have thrown a brick through it. I sit at the dresser and look in the mirror and see the sickness in my face, my thoughts are broken.

"Hey Katie, you fancy a buzz?" Karen says.

"What's that?" I ask.

"It's lighter gas, look you just put this bit in your mouth and push, it's cool, try it!"

I try it and she leaves the room. I remember being told that people's lungs have frozen doing this. I am convinced I am going to die here right in this shitty house. I look in the mirror and say, "You stupid bitch you will die, you will die, don't do this, and don't do this!"

When the buzz wears off I notice that Karen is taking a shit on the floor in the bedroom, the smell mixing in with the rest of the shit.

"What you doing?" I ask.

"Well it's not safe to shit in that toilet and he doesn't use this room. Anyway he just sleeps in his chair by the fire. Come on, let's get out of here, I need to cash his book and get some stuff for him."

"We're aff doon the road James, see you in an hour, alreet?"

"Aye alreet," replies James.

"He doesn't know how much money he gets so I always take a tenner, you know keeps me in fags for the week," says Karen.

While we are down town at the post office I think to myself that it must be sad to live and die in your own shit.

"He doesn't let anyone help him you know," says Karen as if having heard my thoughts.

We get his shopping and a bag of coal so the poor bastard doesn't die of the cold. When we get back we make him a cup of tea and a fire.

When we leave I say, "Poor bastard to die alone in your own

shit, what a fate eh?"

"Yeah, I ken," agrees Karen, "let's go home, yeah?"

"Yeah! That's enough shit for today."

"Welcome to Dysart!" says Karen.

We arrive at the house to the now familiar smell of Shake n' Vac.

"You fancy earning some money?" says Sharon.

"Yeah, how we gonna do that?" I ask.

"There's a woman two doors up who needs a few babysitters for her and her friend at the weekend. We three could do it, all we have to do is pop round at teatime and meet her. What you think, you up for it?" Sharon says.

"Yeah that would be cool, earn some cash n' that like," I say.

Geraldine asks if I could do the hoovering. I agree and get to it. Karen is doing the dishes. I turn the pans of potatoes on to start cooking, thinking I am doing Geraldine a favour, when suddenly she comes bursting into the kitchen.

"You fucking cooking with stoor in the air? You stupid cow, you know you can't cook with stoor in the air, what about my bairn, she'll have it in her dinner."

"What do you mean?" I ask. I have no idea what she is on about.

"Don't fucking 'what' me, you can't fucking cook when the stoor hasny settled; get the fuck out my kitchen!"

"OK," I say. I grab Karen and Sharon and we leave, taking the opportunity to go to visit the babysitting job, leaving Jessie in the house with Geraldine and the baby.

I am still shocked because she smokes around the baby.

We knock on Charley's door; she answers.

"Hello, this is Katie and Karen," says Sharon, "we have come to see about the babysitting at the weekend."

"Come in," says Charley.

As we walk up the stairs a smell of pissy nappies and rubbish hits us; we walk along the hall which is dark with pen drawings courtesy of the kids on the walls. We enter the living room that is sparsely furnished with brown chairs and a bar fire on the wall. The door to the kitchen comes off of the living room; Charley shows us the kitchen which has nothing in it but a kettle and cooker. There is an open bin-bag in the corner which is the obvious source of some of the smells.

"Sorry there is not much in but I am going shopping tomorrow and will buy in some treats for you on Saturday," says Charley.

"So we will be all right for you on Saturday?" asks Sharon.

"Yes that will be fine, how much you want paid?"

"Five pounds per babysitter," says Sharon. "You want us Saturday night, is that right?"

"Yes," says Charley, "is five pound each not a bit too much?"

"You want us to look after four children and one of them is only six months old – that is very cheap," says Karen.

"Yes you are right girls, thank you, I will see you Saturday, OK?"

"See you then," we say and leave.

I didn't want to go to Geraldine's yet as her shouts of stoor were still fresh in my head. I go to the park in the square out the back of the house instead; I'm hanging out with a boy when a loud drunken shout comes from the kitchen window of Geraldine's.

"You fucking slut! Get in here and get your jimmies on," Geraldine roars.

I pass comment on the crazy bitch to the boy and leave. When I arrive in the house Jessie is bent over on the kitchen floor picking up digestives with her hands, a pot of tea was just off the boil on the stove.

"That will teach you to be a smart bitch. You pick all that up in five minutes or I will kick your ass," Geraldine says. "And you," she continues, pointing to me, "sit there."

I sit silently watching in horror from the chair in the living room where I have been instructed to sit, hoping all the time that the attention would not turn to me.

"Stand up!" shouts Geraldine to Jessie.

Jessie stands up.

Geraldine swings her hand and slaps Jessie across the face. "You didn't clean it did you, stupid bitch?" Geraldine is rising, she turns around and grabs the pot of tea and whacks it on Jessie's head. It pours down her back and as Jessie turns to run, Geraldine flings a knife at her; I can see it sticking out of Jessie's ankle. Jessie freezes. All of us freeze, wanting to run but scared of the consequences.

Jessie often peed in the bed and now I understand why. What pressure for a child to live under: the threat of attack any time for the craziest of reasons, today it was a packet of digestives.

"You clean this mess up!" Geraldine is gesturing to me and I step to it as if my life depends on it. "And you," she continues to Jessie, "fuck off out my sight." With this consent Jessie runs to her room for relative safety, for now.

Later that night, Sharon is cleaning her mum's bed when she turns the mattress and finds a folded-up one pound note bang in the middle of the base. She shouts to Geraldine in case her mum is testing her honesty.

"Mum, look what I found under the mattress!" she says to

Geraldine.

"I found one of these the other day exactly like that, there are strange things going on in this house," Geraldine says.

That night Sharon and Karen and I sleep in this bed, we turn off the light and all is quiet.

"Did you hear that?" whispers Sharon.

"Yes!" Karen and I whisper.

"Who's gonna turn on the light?" I say.

"Let's go together," Karen says.

"OK!"

We hold hands and go to switch the light on.

"What's this?" says Sharon, holding out a little coin.

"That's a five shilling," we both say on closer inspection.

"This is freaky," I say. We turn the light out and run to the bed, a few minutes pass and we are all sweating with fear. The room has suddenly turned as cold as ice and we then hear the same sound again.

"Did you hear that?" I whisper to the girls under the covers, we can't bear to look out from under the covers for fear of what we might see.

"Yes."

"Who's going to turn the light on this time? Not me, that's for sure," I say.

"I will go," says Sharon, she is the oldest and has learned many protective instincts living in this home.

The light goes on and Sharon is standing there holding a silver coin; a five shilling. When we look, the one we had previously picked up is still on the dresser. There are now two coins on the dresser. We don't sleep much that night and what sleep we do get is with the lights on. The next day we don't tell Geraldine what had happened and we try to get her to sleep in that room saying we girls wanted to sleep together.

It is Friday now and I have been here for a week and Geraldine has decided in her new good mood to have a few jakie friends around in memory of her mother. We are told that we are to stay in that night; Geraldine's orders are not to be taken lightly. We are all sitting on the sofa in the living room; on the opposite wall the bar fire is on full blast shrouded on each side by old brown units containing Geraldine's glass collection. Karen is sitting on the chair just in front of the unit; I notice a strange kinda greenish-blue smoke coming from the back of the chair. I freak out and start spraying air freshener at the chair with little concern for Karen's head or face.

"What you fucking doing, you crazy bitch?" she asks, completely bewildered.
"I could see blue-green smoke coming from the back of the chair!" I reply back.
"This house is fucking crazy," Karen says.
"What you two up to?" asks Geraldine.
"Nothing, just getting ready for your guests," Karen says.
"Well they will be here soon," Geraldine says. Just then the door goes. Geraldine sits in her seat opposite the smoke chair like a wee queen.
"Get the door, girls." She signals towards the door.
We answer the door to a wrinkled man about 40, his name is Bill.
"Hello lovely girls, how are you today?"
We hold our breath, he smells of alcohol and stale fags.

"We are fine," we say.

There are about ten people in this small living room now. It is incredibly smoky and the drunken oldies are talking shit. If this is what growing up is about I don't want to grow up. I'd rather die young and fuck that shit.

Out of the smell of smoke comes the smell of roses.

"What the fuck?" exclaims Geraldine.

"Who can smell that?"

We wonder if it is a trick question and aren't quite sure how to answer for fear of retribution.

"Roses," says Karen. She is the brave one.

"Yes roses," Geraldine agrees.

Geraldine, Karen, Sharon, Jessie and I can smell the roses but no one else in the room can.

We run about checking all our deodorants and air fresheners, soaps, everything, but nothing smells of this sweet fresh roses smell.

"My mother is happy with her roses," Geraldine says.

It is not long after that Geraldine asks everyone to leave.

"I want to be alone with my thoughts of my mother," she explains.

Everyone leaves and Geraldine goes to bed in the five shilling room. I go in to say goodnight to her. When I enter her room I can see a tall figure in top hat and tails at the end of the bed who almost reaches the ceiling. As I say goodnight it slowly disappears.

I can't sleep, all us girls are now sleeping in the same room and going to the toilet in pairs; all night we can hear noises like the bristles of a hair brush against a heater in the hall, but when we brave a look nothing is there. Roll on tomorrow night, I am babysitting; this house is freaky.

"Get up you lazy bitches!" Geraldine is shouting.

I look through foggy eyes and notice it is only half-eight in the morning.

"Wake up!" Geraldine is shouting.

"Yes Mum," says Karen. It seems Geraldine's pleasant mood has left again.

"Go to the shop, I want rolls and bacon," she bellows.

We get up quick before the punches start to roll out.

"You fucking baby," she shouts at Jessie now as she has wet the bed, "you three fuck off to the shop, I will sort this bitch out."

I leave, feeling sorry for Jessie who is about to take the brunt of Geraldine's early mood.

"We got it like that," says Sharon, "she doesn't do it to us as much anymore, only the odd beat around the head."

"Only?" I question.

We arrive back with the rolls to see Jessie looking battered and Geraldine insisting we stay and have a family breakfast around the table. Jessie is allowed to watch us eat but not eat herself. The smell of bacon must be killing her!

This is a fucked up way of parenting, you want to help her but you know that you will get it if you try. Karen and I pass her some of our bacon when Geraldine is in the kitchen cooking eggs, like she is a nice mother. Surely she must realise the stress she puts on Jessie? Jessie is to be a prisoner of Geraldine's for the day; God knows what is to happen to her today. Karen and I make our excuses and go down to the beach.

"Katie, come here!" Karen shouts.

"What is it?" I ask.

"It looks like a dead seal; look, its eyes have been eaten out," says Karen.

"I have heard about this on the news, there is a seal disease going around, we are supposed to call someone if we find one," I say.

"Phone who?" asks Karen.

"Fuck knows, let's go to the phone box and see if it has anything in it."

At the phone box we call the operator and she gives us the number to call. It doesn't take long for a couple of coastguards to come. They say thank you and remove the seal.

We go back to Geraldine wanting to share our news but when we arrive she is already pissed on vodka and doesn't give a shit.

Jessie is waiting on her hand and foot trying not to anger her.

"We are off to babysit," Sharon tells Geraldine.

"OK," replies Geraldine, too pissed to care.

It is now time to go do our babysitting job so we knock at Charley's door.

"Hello girls, how are you doing?"

"We are fine, you are looking ready to go out, you look nice," says Sharon.

As we walk in the mixture of rotten rubbish, hairspray and perfume is very strange on the senses.

"Here, come and meet my friend, her name is Shona," says Charley.

"Hello girls, thanks for looking after them for us."

"That's fine," Sharon says, "where you going?"

"We are off to Jackie-o's in Kirckleven and we will be back about four in the morning so don't wait up, OK?"

"OK," says Sharon.

"Well let me introduce you to the kids. This is Charlie, he is the youngest at six months, here is Joey he is two years old and Kyle is five," says Charley.

"This is Jessica," says Jennet who is Charley's friend, "she is five as well."

"There is food in the kitchen, just feed Charlie milk and he will be OK," says Charley. Then with that they left.

"Would you believe it, fucking slags, they've only got one box of Weetabix in the cupboard and no milk!" exclaims Sharon. "What the fuck we gonna feed these kids on? We got no money."

"Look, I have found fifty pence in twos and ones on the fireplace, we could get some milk," I say.

"OK you go and get some, we will have to give them all half a Weetabix each and leave it up to them cows in the morning," Sharon says.

It is a long night, the kids are not happy and we are trying to get them into bed. Finally we get them in bed and we get to sleep.

It is morning and the sound of children wakes me up.

"Katie! Katie! They haven't come back!" shouts Karen. "Sharon wake up, they haven't come back!"

"Fuck," says Sharon.

"What the fuck we gonna do? We have no money, no food and four hungry kids," I say.

"I will have to go ask for a tenner from Mum," says Sharon.

"Rather you than me," says Karen.

"You two girls take them to the park," says Sharon, "I will go to Mum's."

We are playing in the park with the hungry children when Sharon arrives.

"She gave me a tenner but we have to pay her back when we get paid," says Sharon.

"Where are they? No phone call, nothing. Karen and I will go to the shops and get food for the house," I say.

"Wait Katie, not so fast, we have to know what we are getting and I am not being left alone with all these children; let's go to their house and figure out a shopping list," Sharon says.

We make the list and I am lucky enough to get to go to the shop as the kids are getting hungrier by the minute which translates into crying and tantrums.

We feed the kids and calm resumes but still no word from the mothers. Sunday night still no word, Monday morning still no word. At lunchtime we receive a call.

"Are the kids all right?" asks Charley.

"Yeah, no thanks to …" then the phone is hung up on me.

They return Tuesday morning, we ask for our payment, a tenner each, and a tenner to cover the food.

"Here, have these," Charley shoves a tenner in my hand.

"What?" I ask.

"We were to have payment each," says Sharon.

"Look, fuck off you or we will kick your cunts in, that's all you're getting," says Jennet who looks like she could kill us!

We leave feeling so pissed at it all but feeling powerless. Karen and I are only 13. Sharon's 15 and all that abuse at home has a weakening effect on your system and we are all knackered from four days of child care.

When we tell Geraldine about it she is so self-righteous about the slags and how they are bad mothers and if it wasn't for her the kids would have starved. It makes her feel like some nice bitch.

"Well girls, where is the money?" Geraldine asks with her hand outstretched. "You are due me a tenner!"

Sharon hands the tenner over with a sigh. All that hard work was for nothing.

"I'm going to the shop," says Geraldine, looking happy with herself. She goes and buys herself a bottle of vodka, coke and some fags.

We are all sat in the living room watching some shit on TV. Geraldine is getting pissed in her chair in the corner which is opposite the TV. Then I notice that there seems to be an exodus of us girls from the room. I quickly join the queue to leave, but just as I am about to leave the room I hear:

"Do I fucking have to sit here on my own?" Geraldine is shouting. I am 30 years old and I have to sit here on my own in my own house? You! Sit the fuck down."

I am officially Geraldine's new prisoner.

"Here girl, pull that chair across, the one near the sofa." She is pointing to the smoky chair so I pull the chair over and sit in it. Geraldine has already moved her vodka and coke to the side of the sofa, the TV is blaring from the right side of me.

"Sit down lassie," she continues, "I want to talk to you." She is talking in a weird 'I'm nice' kinda voice, her breath smells of the toxic mix of vodka and fags and is making me feel sick, but I fear more that this wrinkled old bitch has me prisoner and is uncomfortably close to me.

"You see I love my girls! But the social work department doesn't understand my way of disciplining them," Geraldine says as she swallows more vodka and coke.

"The bastards downstairs lock their children in the bathroom and leave them there while they go out, now that's fucking sick eh Katie, isn't it?"

"Yes," I say, not wanting to say anything that might trigger her anger.

The TV is showing a show about a town where the dogs have rabies. They are savaging all the locals, the locals are then foaming at the mouth, the dogs are foaming at the mouth. I look round and I see Geraldine sorting out all the shit of the day; about how she feels about the death of her mother, about her life and she too is foaming at the mouth. I think I might go crazy tonight.

"I'm going to the toilet," Geraldine says.

I reach for her vodka and drink a big swally. I notice it is 4:00 a.m., then she comes back and this continues till 6:30 in the morning. I am then allowed to go to bed to have a long lie-in till 8:00 a.m.

"Wake up you lazy bitch, you have to go and get rolls for breakfast," says Geraldine, who is obviously immune to the effects of alcohol.

When I am out I call my mum and say I have had enough of a lesson and can I come home. She will need to come get me as I have no money and am too scared to ask Geraldine if I can borrow any. Three hours later my mum arrives and I am glad to leave this nightmare but these girls live with it every day.

CHAPTER 3

Teenage Kicks

It is a usual Sunday at my house; George is watching television with my brother, and I am dozing off in the corner. Suddenly I have a vision of someone running through some woods, the rain beating off their face. I can almost smell the moss under their feet, then as quick as this vision comes, it disappears, leaving me dozing in the warm Sunday vibe of my house.

"I'm going to the bars," I say to my mum. The bars is a place I hang out with my mates, it is all there is in this grey naval estate. The bars are simply bars in concrete at the end of the tarmac path that leads up the hill to my house. They are there to stop people coming down the hill on their bikes and on to the road.

As you come off the roadside through the bars there is a brown wooden slatted fence to the right. All the rubbish, fag wrappers and butts are glued together with the dirt and piss pushed against the bottom of the fence like smelly miniature mountains of grime, forged by the winds that come in from the left. On the left hand side there is a wire fence with diamond shapes that let in all the eerie sounds as the winds pass the grey boarded-up box-like naval flats.

The bin stores with their rattling doors hanging off, the faint sound from the movement of the millions of pieces of broken glass in the disused drying green and the smell of piss in the air is what greets me as I arrive to meet my friends.

Louise, Gerome, Jason and Karen are all there. "Alreet?" says Jason, "how's it going?"
"Just hanging out at my mum's, you know, Sunday dinner, racing on TV, boring; thought I would come and see what's

going on, anything happening?"

"Na, fuck all," says Jason. Louise broke in, "There is a party at Maggie's hoose, you up for it?" Maggie is an older woman that lives on the naval estate. She likes having all us young ones at her hoose, she gets us alcohol.

"When is it, like?" Gerome asks.

"Next Saturday night," Louise replies.

"I'm gony need te try and scam to get there," I say.

"Yeah! I ken me an' aw," says Karen. "What are you gon' tell your ma?"

"I'm gonni tell her I'm staying at Nia's hoose."

"Who is Nia?" asks Karen.

"She's a friend of mine from up toon, my ma weny mind if I stay there. I will ask her after school the morrow. Anyway I better be going hame and get ready, I still have dishes to do or I'm gonna be grounded next Saturday, see ya!" I say.

"See you on the bus the morrow," they all shout.

The week passes by fast. The bell rings as usual on Friday afternoon. I run to the school bus; on the bus is the usual chaos. The smell of sweaty teenage boys and bubblegum, the condensation from the concoction of breaths on the windows, the hard maroon leather seats torn and teased until their very stuffing, fluffy and white, is exposed and the noise of 50 excited children high on freedom and E-numbers from the sweets which they are liberally spreading around the bus.

I look around for my friends, passing the first years at the front of the bus (I remember being a first year and how freaky it was), then on past the middle and there is Louise just before the back of the bus. She has kept me a seat. "You coming to the party the morrow?" she asks as I sit down.

"What party?" shouts a voice from Dudley, a spotty-nosed boy from Rothsy (a village not far from my home). "Nene of your fucking business," shouts Louise.

"Yeah I'm coming. I managed to scam my mother into thinking that I am staying at Nia's hoose; she thinks I'm gony get the bus at 5:00 p.m. then I will come and meet you at the bars."

"The party's no' starting till eight o'clock," says Louise. "Yeah! I thought so but this is tough." The bus stops at Dudley's stop, he hits me on the back of the head as he passes me saying, "Fucking dockyard slut," then he gets off the bus. (It is a common lie that any girl who lives in the dockyard naval estate is a slut because of the navy's reputation, also continuing rumours among them that prostitutes work there.) Finally I reach my stop. "See you later at the bars about five/half five, all right?"

"Yeah! See you later," says Louise.

I have some dinner then disappear up to my room to get my party gear ready and well stashed in my bag. "See you later Mum I'm off to Nia's," I shout as I rush down the stairs and nearly out the door – oops, stuck in no-man's-land again. "Come here Katie and give me a kiss goodbye. You remember – NO drinking, NO silly business and straight there and back, OK?"

"OK Mum, love you, see you tomorrow," and with that said, off I go to the bars with a party in my mind and just the right party gear in my bag.

"What you wearing?" asks Louise.

"Just some jeans and that wee black top of mine, do you think we could go to Maggie's earlier and get ready? You know, get our hair done, make-up on! I didny have a chance at mine, would have been sussed straight away."

"Let's go and see, she can only say no," says Louise. We knock on Maggie's door with a little apprehension hoping that we won't be turned away. "Hello Maggie how's it going? You all right?" I say. "All right girls I'm no' bad, it's a bit early is it no'?" "Yes, sorry about that," says Louise, "we were just wondering if it would be all right if we came in and done our hair and make-up here?"

"Nae bother girls, just come in." She steps aside and in we go. Her house is an average naval house, her husband is away. As you walk into the hall it is dark and smoky, the stairs are on the left with white gloss paint tinted yellow with smoke, on the left is the kitchen door then straight ahead is the living room door. "On you go girls, just go in the living room."

As you enter the living room there is a big mahogany cabinet along the left wall and the curtains are closed. In the far right corner is a dinner table behind a blue sofa and chair which are divided by a coffee table. The living room has a door off to the right that leads to the kitchen and from the kitchen a door back into the hall. It's very smoky but we don't mind as we both smoke as well. Finally, some warmth and comfort to smoke a fag in rather than at the bars.

"How you gonna do your hair?" Maggie asks me. "I reckon I will put mine in a ponytail and backcomb the fringe." "And you Louise, what you gonna do?" "I think I will just blow-dry it with the diffuser, oh that's if you have one?" "Yes I do," replies Maggie. "Come here I will get it for you, oh I must be going fucking daft, you fancy a drink?" "Yes please!" we both say in chorus, "what you got?" "I've nearly got enough to open a liquor store; there is whisky, Southern Comfort, Malibu, vodka or Baileys. Oh, and yes, lemonade, beer, Irn Bru and Coca-Cola. What you fancy getting bevyed on the night girls?"

"Wow," I reply, "what a selection! I fancy havin' a vodka and coke please."

"I fancy havin' a vodka and Irn Bru please," Louise says.

"Well I tell you what," says Maggie, "if you help yourself I will get the hair dryer."

"OK thanks," we both reply.

"That's nae bother, girls," says Maggie.

The door goes, so I go and answer it. Standing there are two guys, one is called Kyle and his mate is called Daniel.

"All right how's it going guys?" I say.

"We're good, just got leave for the weekend." (They are both sailors.)

"You guys are ready to fucking party?"

"You bet!!"

"Well there's some drinks in the kitchen, help yourselves, there is a wide selection to choose from or if you fancy I denny mind pouring them for ye."

"Well hmmm! I think a whisky would be good for me," Kyle says.

"I'll have a beer," says Daniel.

The door goes again and the guests start arriving. Next to arrive are Nancy, Karen and big Louise.

"Come in and get yourself a drink," I say, trying to be the hostess with the mostest! The party is in full swing by now, people are bringing all sorts of alcohol. People are starting to get drunk, dancing, canoodling and generally letting loose, Saturday night style.

Nancy comes in and says to me, "He's gorgeous! Don't you think?" (referring to Kyle).

"Ah! He's no' bad but I'm not that interested in him." "I am," she replies, "I fancy him, what do you think my chances?"

"Don't know," I say, "go give it a shot!"

Some time passes and next thing I know there is a fight; I'm not sure what is happening but I realise Kyle is on the street outside. I go out to see if he is all right, Daniel was well gone due to too much mixing drinks.

"Are you alreet?" I ask Kyle.

"Yeh! I will be fine, will just go back to base." Then I hear the drunken voice of Maggie shouting from the house with Nancy standing behind her. "Fuck off you slut, if you want to talk to that stupid bastard you don't come back in here," she is shouting to me.

"Shit," I say, "what the fuck happened there?"

"Maggie was trying to get off with me, I turned her down, she wasn't too happy, then that wee bitch Nancy stirred her up."

"I'm fucked! I can't go home to my parents. I lied about where I was going and I won't be able to go back till eight or nine in the morning. Fuck! What am I gonna do?"

"I will hang out with you, let's take a walk, get away before they phone the police. I am sorry to get you chucked out of the party!"

"It's all right, what are friends for? I just wanted to know you were all right and what had happened," I say.

"Where shall we go? I don't know around here," says Kyle.

"Well there are some woods down there, it is getting light, me and my mates hang out there all the time, there is a tree swing."

"That sounds good; it's not far from base, I can easy get back when you get to go home."

"Thanks Kyle!"

"That's OK, what are friends for?"

So we walk to the tree swing and start to play. The swing is over a big crevice, at the bottom there is only dirt and rocks edged off with green bushes and nettles; it is great fun to feel the fear as you jump on to the swing and go speeding over it and back. Then it starts to rain.

"What shall we do?" I ask Kyle.

"Let's take some shelter under this bush, I'm sure the rain will pass." He signals to a bush just up from the tree swing which is under a large tree; there isn't much space there but the bush is dense and affords us some shelter from the rain. We climb under it and try to tread down some nettles and manage to clear us a space, it smells of moss, rotting leaves and dampness.

"This is shit! I only came out for a second to see how you were. They knew I couldn't go home."

"Am sorry about that," he says. We huddle together to keep warm and dry. Then I feel him starting to kiss my cheek.

"We are friends," I emphasise, "I just want to keep warm."

"This will keep us warm," he replies.

"What are you doing? Please stop it! Leave me alone, just chill, we are just friends, OK?"

"It's all right, you know you want it girl!"

"You're hurting my tits, I want you to leave me alone!"

"What's wrong? We are just wasting some time."

"I don't want this!" I try to make a break for the rainy woods not knowing where I can go. He is in front of my only way out. I look around, there is no clearing around me; as I turn around to face him I feel him slowly pushing me backwards till I am lying down. The pressure of him on top of me pushing me deep into the bush, his belt pushing into my pubic bone.

"STOP!!!" I yell, "I don't want to!" I feel all my strength being pushed out of me. "Stop!" My voice becomes weak as I know it is futile to protest.

"Come on girl, it will be nice, you will like it."

I disappear inside my head; the pressure on my body is immense. I can't move, I just feel pain around my fanny. I am silently crying tears like rain flowing down my cheeks. I can feel his breath hot on my face as he is thrusting himself hard into me and laying his full pressure on all my body. Between my legs I feel wet, he pulls away.

"See, that was fine wasn't it?" he asks.

I slowly pull my jeans up and start doing them up.

"Why are you crying? You wanted it."

"I am going home now," I reply quietly.

"But it's too early, your parents will kill you for lying to them!"

"I don't care anymore," I say weakly.

"Suit yourself, I will call on you on Wednesday," he says.

I am running through the woods, the rain beating off my face mixing in with my tears, my fear and my shock.

It smells wet and damp; the moss is soft under my feet causing me to lose balance.

I am cold, lonely, dirty and scared. I seem to be tripping on things that don't exist. Suddenly the cover of the woods is gone and I am on the roadside. The rain is beating down and as I look up I see the concrete hill stretched out before me and the omnipresent naval estate on which I live.

It's too early to go in so I sit on the steps in the back garden trying not to cry aloud. If I wake my parents up they will know that I have been lying to them.

I don't know what time it is but I feel like I have been sitting here for hours.

I am in shock. What just happened? What just happened? I feel myself, I am sore and wet. I feel dirty; "Fucking slut," I hear me telling myself.

My mind is going crazy, I must pull myself together, I must go in looking OK. I can't bear it anymore, must go in the house, so I knock on the door. My mother answers.

"Hello you are early!" she says.

"Yes I know," (I try to sound all right) "I am going to my room, me and Nia had an argument." I go to my room; when I enter the room my bed is there as I had left it the night before covered with all the change of clothes, my drawers left half-open and my stereo on top of them.

The window is showing the sunrise, it smells of my perfume and talc, a soft smell, it feels safe and familiar in here but my body doesn't.

I am hollow, empty, and confused. What just happened? I immediately start to pour a bath. Then I take off my knickers, they are wet with this slimy stuff, I am bruised around my inner thighs and hips, 'must have been his belt' I think. BASTARD!! My legs are itchy, they are stung all over with nettle stings, must have been nettles everywhere. BASTARD!! I feel minging.

"Are you all right?" My mum shouts from downstairs.

"Aye I'm no' bad, just having a bath!"

"Didn't you have one at Nia's?"

"Na I just left, I couldny be bothered, have had enough of her shit, I just left."

I soak in the bath and put my clothes in the wash then pull myself together and go downstairs.

"What's wrong Katie? You don't seem yourself, why are you washing up and bathing and tidying, it is not like you? My God, you have even put a wash on! There must be something wrong."

"Nothing's wrong I'm just tired."

"How could you get back from Nia's so early? Did her mum know you were gone?"

"No I sneaked oot," I say, trying to cover my tracks but I don't have much clear thought.

"I will phone her mum, she will be worried what has happened to you."

"NO!!! Ye denny hav'te do that."

"Why? Katie, are you lying to me? Where were you last night? The first bus didn't start until after you had arrived."

"OK! I lied, I went to a party!"

"Where and with who?"

"I denny want to tell you."

"I don't care," her voice is now rising, "you have no choice, tell me now."

"It was at Maggie's house."

"Who is Maggie?"

"She is a lady who has a flat on the estate."

"Was there alcohol there?"

"Yes!"

"How old is she?"

"About thirty."

"Thirty! What the fuck has she got a load of teenagers drinking in her house for? Did you drink?"

"Aye a wee bit," I say.

"Right, you are grounded," shouts my stepfather George.

"OK nae bother to me," I say.

"Anything could have happened to you," says my mother.

"I ken."

"You are too young for all this, Katie"

"I ken I'm sorry eh."

"What's happened? You never agree with me, something must have happened? What's wrong?"

"I denny ken." I start to cry.

"What's fucking up with her?" asks George.

"I don't know, come to my room Katie, let's talk," says my mum.

"Fucking lying bitch, she will be grounded for a month."

"Shut up George!" my mum says, "something is wrong."

We are in my mum's bedroom now.

"Tell me what happened," Mum says softly, "it's not like you to agree with me. What has happened?"

"I'm not sure, I feel so bad and this guy…" I stop trying to figure out what just happened to me and what to say.

"What guy? What happened? You can tell me, I am here for you, Katie."

"This guy who is meant to be a friend," I proceed to tell her the story of when I left the party, "well, he forced himself on me."

"What do you mean he forced himself on you?" She had more urgency in her voice now.

"I don't know," I say, becoming more distressed, "he pushed me down in the woods."

"The woods?" my mum interrupts, "I thought you were at a party."

"I told you we were flung out the party! Well he was; I kept saying 'What are friends for?' I kept saying I didn't want this!"

"Want what?" My mum is speaking very softly now.

"They wouldny let me back in the party."

"Who's they?"

"Maggie and Nancy."

"What happened?" Mum asks quietly.

"He said 'Thanks for helping me', I said 'What are friends for? I kept saying 'friends'."

"Let me help you Katie, please, you need to tell me what happened."

So I tell her what had happened in the woods, I show her my bruises and stings.

"You have been raped, Katie."

Finally this gives me some definition as to what has just happened to me; I know I had said no loads of times, but I didn't understand what had just happened to me.

"Who is this guy?" asks Mum.

"His name is Kyle."

"How old is he? Where is he from?" she asks.

"He's 19 and he is a sailor."

"We must take you to the police, Katie."

"Why, what for?" I start to get worried.

"They will have to gather evidence to catch him. You have had a bath haven't you?"

"I have, yes," I say.

My mum proceeds to phone the police and we are asked to go in and see a police doctor.

At the police station I am taken to speak to a policewoman.

They take me into a room with one office table in it and a chair either side; the walls are painted with washable mint green paint.

The policewoman starts to ask me some questions about what has happened to me.

My mum is by my side helping me out by supporting me, holding my hand as step by step I relive my trauma.

"We can only help you if you tell us the truth, Miss Brown," the police officer says, pressing me for more details.

I don't want to live through all this again and again.

Then she says, "OK Miss Brown, we will now take you to the police doctor, he will perform a few procedures to obtain more evidence."

"Do I have to?" I reply.

"Well you may choose to refuse but without this procedure there will not be any evidence to charge your attacker."

"Hello Miss Brown, welcome, my name is Doctor Baxter. I am the police doctor, I am going to have to perform some routine procedures. What I will have to do is take a sample of your hair from your head, also your pubic hair, this is in case your attacker has left any semen behind. I will also have to take a vaginal smear. This is also to see if he has left any semen inside you. I understand you have had a bath, this will significantly reduce any evidence. Your mother has already phoned home to find the clothes you were wearing. Would you please take off your clothes and lie on the bed behind the screen."

I do as I am told and proceed to take off my clothes. This is shit; I always said if it ever it happened to me I would never have a bath, I would rake at the bastard with my nails and I would never wash my clothes. The strange thing is now it is happening to me all I can think of is to wash him away. So I continue this nightmare and put on their robe and lie on the bed waiting for the next attack.

"Can I ask you to raise your legs and part them please?"

He positions my legs, my vagina feels the cold air and I feel the trauma and embarrassment once again.

"I am just going to pop this speculum inside you," he says. "Please relax, try and think of something nice."

I laugh in disbelief. 'Think of something nice!' – and how am I supposed to do that? I tell my mum I will think of a nice warm beach. She holds my hand to try to comfort me.

My imagination is shattered. "Ouch!" I let out, as this cold plastic speculum is inserted into my bruised vagina. I feel this horrible scraping feeling.

"I am just taking some swabs of your vagina wall, one at the front and one at the top. Hold on, that's it you can relax for a minute," he says as he pulls the speculum out from inside me.

"I will just need to take a pubic hair sample," he says, "hold on, this might be nippy."

"Ouch!!" I cry in pain as he pulls out some hair at the root from my bruised pubic area. I lie there feeling violated and weak once more. I disappear inside my head and the tears began to fall silently down my face. What is happening to me?

I am back home now alone in my room crying. I have been here for a few days. I'm not hungry and don't want to eat, don't want to speak, don't want to ever go back to school. I just want this confusion and hate to go away.

Suddenly the door bursts open and in flies George. "**FUCKING SHUT UP!**" he shouts. "You have been crying for days, is it not about time you shut your mouth? It happened; all right you just have to get over it – and another thing, you will be going to school tomorrow. I have had enough of you, you fucking melodramatic bitch." This makes me cry even more!

So here I am waiting at the bus stop with tracky bottoms covering my legs.

"Fucking slut!" a voice says. It is Nancy.

"Kyle didn't rape you, you asked for it, you fucking slut."

"Just wait till after school, you are getting what you deserve, you lying bitch. Get my mate in trouble like that."

"He has told us all about it, you lying to the police, you wee bitch."

I am numb. The bus arrives and my body gets on but I seem to have lost my soul. I sit at the front trying to avoid more verbal abuse but this fails. Everyone knows what happened and I feel like this is hell on earth. I denny think I will survive school today. It seems like an eternity for the bus to get to school and when it stops I am one of the first ones off and I make haste to my classroom.

I am waiting outside one of my classes feeling like shit; I feel so alone and, dare I say it, vulnerable.

"There's the fucking slut!" a voice says. It is Nancy again but with her friends this time.

"See you after school!" they shout as they pass.

I am a pushover, I have no strength even to react; he has damaged my life's energy.

I am at the bus stop at school waiting to get the bus home, I have fear in me but am really too numb to acknowledge it.

Who cares anyway? My stepdad says I'm a bitch n' slut, so do the people at school. Maybe this is the case; it is true I am a worthless slut.

I don't even care if they kick my head in so hard I die because life is full of shit.

My fate is closing in, here comes the bus, just a wee torturous journey then the end, thank fuck. I have had enough.

The bus is suitably packed for the occasion, many people who live in the town have come to see the execution of the slut who asked for it then complained.

The bus is pulling up at my stop. I hear the chant of "Fight! Fight!! Fight!!!"

I don't want to look back and face my fate so I slowly walk off the bus, pass the bars and up the tarmac path that leads to my house.

I want to run but can't. I'm numb to all of this. I keep walking, not turning back. I can hear the crowd gathering and the continual chants of "Fight! Fight! Fight!"

"Turn around, you fucking slag," says the leader, a six-foot girl with black hair, she is called Louise, she's solid. I can hear that Nancy is somewhere behind her. "Fucking turn around bitch, are you chicken?"

I keep walking, I don't want to turn around to face my hospitalisation.

"You fucking slag, you lied, Kyle never done anything, he said you were begging him for it. Now you are trying to get him in trouble. He's too nice, he wouldn't do that," says Nancy.

I quietly say, "Just cos you fancy him."

"I don't know what you're fucking saying, slag," Louise breaks in.

I can feel the gap between us getting smaller and smaller but I can't move from my fate. Suddenly I feel this heavy weight on my body; a punch to the face, my mouth fills with the iron taste of blood. It has begun.

I am surrounded. Fight! Fight! Fight!

Kicks start laying into my already bruised body. I lie in the foetal position, the tarmac unforgiving, pushing into my face, the faint smell of piss. I take the abuse, tears silently falling down my face.

"Leave the slag alone," says Louise. One more kick comes. "Bitch," I hear Nancy say.

I lie there for a time, I don't know how long for, then I drag myself home.

"What the fuck happened to you?" George shouts.

"Nothing," I say.

"Don't look like nothing to me!"

"Just a beating for being a slut and lying about Kyle, it dosny matter."

"Go tidy yourself up, it always looks worse before that."

I am now cleaned and in my room. Time eludes me now and I can't gauge how long I have taken to get here. I feel nothing but this big empty shell of a wounded body.

"Katie," shouts George, "come downstairs, I have to go and pick your mother up," he continues. "Leona is in her bed. Look after her for a bit, I won't be long, bye!" (Leona is my eight-month-old niece.) As soon as he leaves, my mind returns to a vacant place. I have no memory of what has just been said; to me there is only white noise and numbness in my brain.

I sit down on the sofa and lean over on the coffee table in the living room. As I open my eyes in the mist of tears I see a notepad and pen through the glass top of the table. The day's events start to run through my head. My head is sore; my face, my body, my heart all wounded. I will write it down then they will see it is true.

I start to write about the rape, I want to purge my system. I write about Kyle –the bastard, I did say no. He took my virginity; I didn't want that, it did happen.

I know it happened and why I feel so bad; everything that happened pours out on to the page.

I have found a razor by now and I am cutting the top of my arm; I don't want to kill myself, just bleed on my words to show my sincerity. The pain is sweet relief, kinda like a steam valve letting off, blood immortalising my every word. This will surely show everyone the truth; this is what happened to me.

I am now in a strange trance; I find myself reaching for George's drinks cabinet, it is right in front of me, it is calling to me. Strong spirits – whisky, Harvey's Bristol Cream – one by one they flow down my throat like water. It is easier to cut now that I feel no pain.

No feeling when I am like this, yes! I will have more, ah! There are some pills also in the cabinet; one by one they are sent down my throat with waves of alcohol, and it's easier to gulp the strong booze as time passes.

Pages of truth, of abuse, are written getting less legible all the time. The booze and pills are slipping down my throat and nothing seems to matter anymore, I'm not sure where I am but I feel fine. I am slipping into completeness. Numb, totally numb. Ah, what relief this is not to care, not to feel.

I am getting really dizzy now; something is pulling at me, something keeps pulling at my senses. I am hearing something ask me a question: "You want to die? You really want to die? You are slipping, DO YOU WANT TO DIE???" "NO!! NO!! NO!!" I find myself shouting. Before I know it, I am on the phone to my friend. "Help me!! I have taken some pills and I think I am going to die!"

"Come to my house quick," she says. Her name is Magda.

I really don't know how I got here but I am now in her house and her mother has phoned an ambulance and is now calling George.

"Your daughter is here, she has a taken an overdose, I have called an ambulance."

"Send her home!" he shouts down the phone.

"Send her home, what do you mean 'send her home'? She can't walk, you need to come down here now."

She turns to me and says, "Don't go to sleep, you have to walk around until the ambulance comes here."

"But can't I just have a wee rest, I am a wee bitty tired?" I reply.

"No don't. Magda, keep her awake," she says to her daughter.

"Here is the ambulance, where is that prick George? His daughter is here dying and he is not here."

Magda helps me into the ambulance.

"You can't let her sleep, OK?" says the ambulance attendant as she climbs into the ambulance with us.

"Katie!" shouts Magda, "you can't sleep, tell me something, stay awake, sit up, you're falling."

I am laughing and making jokes, getting a bit crazy. "Just a wee rest," I say.

"NO! Wake up!" Magda is getting stressed. "Don't stress baby."

I say, "I'm fine, it's warm in here isn't it?"

We arrive at the hospital, I am put on a trolley. The world is spinning and there is lots of talking and then I am in the hospital, I see the ceiling lighting above me; I pass out.

"Ahh!! Get off me!!!"

"Katie, you have passed out," says a voice of a doctor standing above my head.

"Get off me, why am I tied down? Let me go, you are trying to kill me."

"We are trying to help you, Katie, calm down, we are going to pump your stomach."

"Arge! Arge!" This big fat tube is being forced down my throat; I tear my restraints and pull the tube out of my throat.

"You are going to kill me!"

"Please stay calm, you will be in trouble if you don't get those pills out of your system. OK," says the doctor, "there is one other option open to us."

"What is it?" my mum asks with urgency.

"I have the option of some medicine that you drink, it will make you sick; you also need an injection."

"OK, here is a good vein, I've seen this in the movies, here, just here." I am pointing to a vein in my arm. The doctor injects me in a vein in my hand and then gives me the liquid medicine.

"Arge!" I am now being violently sick, sick like there is no tomorrow. The next thing I know I am lying in bed in a strange place.

I look around the ward across from me; around me are all sick old women. They must have put me in the wrong ward. One of the women is getting her hair done by a nurse.

"Here you are Mrs Riley, would you like two plaits or one?"

"Just one my dear," she replies.

Another nurse says, "Time for your medicine, Mrs Riley."

"Do you think I am crazy? You are trying to kill me, you don't take pills at the hairdressers," Mrs Riley shouts.

"Nurse!" I shout. "Where am I?"

"You are in the constant care unit, Ward 43."

"Why am I here?"

"Because you tried to commit suicide, you are under constant supervision should you try and do this again."

"Why would I do that?"

"I am sure you will not," replies the nurse, "though I must tell you that you are not permitted to close the curtains around your bed. The toilets are over there to the right. You are allowed to smoke but only in the TV room which is two doors down from the toilet."

It is night now and I can't sleep. I don't like it here, I am not supposed to be here, I lie dozing then finally sleep comes. Suddenly I am woken up with a start. "You stole my clothes," an old lady is shouting as she empties out my locker pulling all my clothes on the floor.

"Fuck off you crazy old bitch, I have nothing of yours. Nurse, nurse!"

The nurse comes and manages to settle the woman down in her bed. I am determined that I will leave this ward tomorrow.

Tomorrow comes with no such luck for me; I have been told I am not allowed to leave until I see a psychiatrist and she is not available till tomorrow. Another night on this crazy ward for me, they say they want to make sure I will not try and commit suicide again. "Why the fuck you think I'm going to do that again?" I reply. "Do you think I want to visit this shit hole full of crazy people again?"

"Now there is no need for this language, I will have you kept in for another day if you do not calm down. The police will not let you leave unless we are sure you will not be back."

So another crazy night of snoring old biddies. I look around me as sleep will not come and I am not allowed to close my curtains. There is the woman in front, you know, the hairdresser woman, she looks dead, she has white hair and is bolt upright with her mouth wide open. Next to her are other old women with their life barely in them, connected to drips and colostomy bags. This is not going to help my fear of old age if I had any. There is one woman on a bed behind that and she freaks me out, she is always fitting and she rattles constantly, she shouts and swears. These people are crazy. I will need counselling for just being in here. Why did they put me in here?

I wake up; I am not sure when sleep came to claim me but I am still tired.

"Miss Brown," a voice of a nurse says.

"What?" I say, startled. "Why did you get me up so early?"

"Everyone has to get up, my dear. It's your leaving day today. I see you are going to talk to our psychiatrist, she is a lovely woman."

"Yeah, whatever." My reply is tired and lacking any lustre for the meeting of this so-called nice psychiatrist.

I arrive in the hospital's psychiatrists' room. It is minging yellow and the tarred carpets are certainly not inviting. The woman is called Sara.

"Hello Katie, have a seat." She gestures towards a hard chair in the corner then she sits just opposite me.

"Miss Brown, do you know how serious what you have just done is?"

I am now thinking 'not another night in here' so I answer with what I feel she will want to hear. "Yes," I reply.

"We have to come to some agreement," she continues. "You have two choices: either you agree to talk with a counsellor about the reasons why you tried to take your own life or you will have to go into care where there will be a constant eye kept on you."

"Wow, what a choice," I say sarcastically, "I will go and see a counsellor. Can I go home now?"

"Your mother is here to collect you. I must stress to you if you do not attend the appointments with the counsellor there will be a meeting to review your care options."

'That meeting should take a while' I think.

"Thanks a lot," I say arrogantly. My mum comes and I leave for home. I am scared. I don't want to see George. I fucking hate him.

Next Monday is the day I have my appointment with the counsellor, my mum takes me and says she will come to pick me up.

The office is in Dunfress and it's not far away from the train station and a good park. I am already spotting ways to skive these appointments because I know this was bullshit; I just need peace, I know what is best for me as I am 15 years old, I am not a child anymore.

"Hello," says this lady in her mid-forties with a bad hairdo and musty clothes. "My name is Mrs Peasbody, I am your counsellor, please follow me."

I follow her up the stairs where she opens the door to an office that is just as musty as her. There is a wee window at the right as I go in; there is a chair either side of it. To me it does not spell comfort or security, it spells 'come on, get it out'. I fear it is somewhere I am not ready to go to.

The sun is beating in the window and there seems to be increasingly less air to breathe.

"Please take a seat." She gestures towards the den of hell which I see before me. I'm definitely a closed book and no one is going to take me back to where I have just been.

"Well Katie, I am here to help you."

"I am fine," I reply abruptly.

"Well, we have an hour so why don't we take a little time to get to know each other? I hear you have been through quite a traumatic time lately, would you like to tell me something that you are feeling? It is always good to share things, they are better when talked about with support."

"I suppose so," I reply, not convincing anyone. I have no idea where to begin.

"Shall we start at the beginning?" she says, as if reading my mind.

I start to tell her about the party, this is the easy part to talk about. I stop as if something just choked me, words sticking in my throat mixed up with the ball of tears and pain trying to get out, even though I am trying not to let it.

I am angry with myself, I have cried enough, surely. George's words ringing in my head, "Melodramatic bitch, have you not cried enough?"

I hear her voice, "It is all right Katie, you are safe now. I am here, you are not alone."

No, it is impossible, I can say no more. The thought of him forcing his fucking penis inside me is making me sick. I am angry and confused, I hear the voices of the gang that battered me saying, "Slut, slag you wanted it." It is all too much for me.

"I can't do this." I run out of the room. I run down the street to the empty park. What a waste of time, it just makes me cry and relive the pain again. It is like being raped three times: once by the bastard himself, once by the police doctor and once by the counsellor.

Fuck them, fuck them all. Every appointment after that I pretend to go to the counsellor. I wave goodbye to my mum as she drops me off and then I go to the park for an hour. It is a much less painful experience than I thought it would be, for I know now that I am not going to kill myself, it seems death is not my way out.

CHAPTER 4

Short Stay at the Holiday inn

I have arrived at the hostel in which I have been forced to stay. George had told me he was going to kick me out but he was going to tell me where to go.

"Here is your room Miss Brown," says the hostel attendant. I walk into this dark room with one window overlooking the bus station. I have regulation furniture: one soft chair, one hard chair, one desk, a wardrobe, a bed and a sink. The carpet is tarred to the floor and it is of a ridged kind. The colour scheme is a deep red with magnolia walls. I notice the Blu-tak marks of the previous occupant. A shudder of fear and horror comes over me. This will be my home.

I am officially on my own as my parents have washed their hands of me. The hostel will receive my benefits money as I am not old enough to deal with the paying of rent. It will be £115 per week for this poky shit hole. I will receive £40 per week to live on and I must attend school or this money will be taken away from me. I have a lock on my door that is not allowed to be locked to allow 24-hour access to hostel staff. This freaks me out. I am to share this flat with one other girl, a fruitcake called Sasha. I am now officially my own guardian at the tender age of 15.

Sasha, my new flat mate, comes in; she is excited to see me but I have absolutely no joy for her whatsoever.
"I like it here," she says, "the staff are really nice and they take me shopping and help me cook."
"Bully for you," I reply and enter my room and close the door in her face.
In my room alone I am in shock; I feel vulnerable with the stark

realisation that I will not be going home; 15 years old and alone in a hostel full of weirdos. On top of that I have to go to school which I hate; I feel I have enough on my plate without that shit.

Monday comes; Jimmy, one of the hostel workers comes to my flat and says he is going to take me to cash my book and show me how to shop for a week's food. I cash the £155 and I feel rich, and think maybe it's OK being your own guardian. I got my own money, no more begging George for a fiver. I am taken around some shops and the last thing I want to do is spend my money on food. I want new shoes and clothes, but I am held back by Jimmy who says you can't eat shoes. I am back at the hostel now and we are in the office; this is painful, I have to hand over £115 to the hostel and I get a receipt that my rent is paid. They then point out I should go and get ready to go to school. I am in my room and school is the last thing on my mind. It has already been pointed out to me that if I don't go I will lose my place in the hostel, so off I go.

It takes me a few days then I realise that I am my own guardian, I don't need to answer to anyone. The next week I take a few days off and write myself a wee note for the teachers. It says 'Katie was off because Katie was ill, yours sincerely Katie'.

I am home now and sitting in the living room kitchen in my shared flat. Sasha comes in and asks, "How was your day? Did they take you shopping? They do that with everyone."
"Do they?" I reply back. I tell her that I was supposed to go shop for a meal and cook it for Jimmy the hostel attendant to show him that I am capable of doing this. He does not turn up for this meal the next night; this pisses me right off, never again

am I going to waste my time on their shit. I will attend school the bare minimum so as not to get my money stopped and that would be it. Sasha has her own story to tell. She has had it hard she tells me. One night she has been abused by her uncle, father and several of his mates, they had beaten her and gang-raped her on several occasions and because of the beatings damaged her brain as they were so severe. I wonder with despair at how sick humans can be towards other fellow humans. Where is the love in this world?

There is a party at Logger's room today and we are busy brewing mushrooms. We have all been down the glen every day for a week collecting them. This brew has about 25,000 mushrooms and should be a brew to remember. I have noticed that being on my own is teaching me things other than how to shop for food and pay rent; it is teaching me how to get severely wasted. It is a very well-thought-out affair. I am learning how to get alcohol bought for me and how to allocate money for dope, acid, speed, parties and all sorts.

I have gone down to Logger's and am helping prepare the room for the coming guests. I close all the windows and put a damp towel at the bedroom door. We have put bottles of open poppers at many points around the room and then start the techno music. The vibe is getting exciting. I ask Logger, "Why the towel at the door?" He replies that as we are going to smoke a power of dope it will stop it setting off the smoke alarms. That reminds me, I better get out the bong. Logger is a guy with dreads about seven years older than me. He is always making tin drum kits out of old baked beans cans and matchsticks then painting them black. We have about four ounces of dope and plenty of drink, especially Buckfast. The mushies are brewing steadily and people are now arriving, bringing wine, beer, more dope. "Let's get bended!" Logger shouts.

Everyone agrees and the party is starting. The bong is loaded and we start the smoking. There are about 20 of us now and we are all getting well bended, talking about the cons of the day or week, and I have learned a lot on how to con the systems that exist in this world. The room by now is so smoky that my eyes are watering. Then the door opens and in comes Logger and his mate with this wicked mushroom brew. We are all up for it and there is also a sense that if you don't join in the fun provided you can then leave now or suffer the consequences.

Everyone has a cup of the brew. We are sharing mugs around one by one and we are getting bended more and more by the second. The sweet, muddy, milky taste is strange to me but I am stoned and munched and sweet tastes are always good in this state. In no time at all the room is starting to look crazy. The smoke is moving around us, people's conversations are becoming weird. My friends' faces are bending and twisting till I have to blink in disbelief. I feel as though I am drifting into the corner of the room and I think to myself that this is a mind-bender. I am not sure whether I am enjoying it or not when I feel a hand holding mine. "Are you all right?" asks a voice. It is Jackie who is a new friend I have made, about five years older than me. "Katie I am here, are you all right?" she asks again.

"Come in here with me Jackie, it's great, it's colourful." As she holds my hand we disappear into a vortex of colours spinning around in my mind but it seems like reality. Jackie flows with me, she is a dab hand at this tripping business, I like her, she has a good mentality. In the distance I hear the sound of the door bell ringing and suddenly I am back in the room. The people in the room start singing, "Will somebody get the door, will somebody get the door!" I look around me and there are loads of familiar faces with wee trippy twists smoking bongs and joints, drinking, laughing. One guy gets up. "I'm going to the door," he says. When he comes back we ask who is at the door. He says, "24 spaceships," then sits down. Time is immeasurable, the thought of who is really at the door left me. I look up and one guy called Lil Jim bursts open the window and shouts, "Fuck off don't shoot me," and runs out the window. There is a slight discussion about someone going after him and we all decided na, leave him, we would have a bong and that he would be all right.

The music is becoming mind-bending and I can faintly smell the poppers over the smell of smoke. There is a strange ringing that seems to be constant and it suddenly dawns on us that it is the fire alarm. We have smoked so much the wet towel is not enough to hold it back from seeping under the door. People start to jump out the window. Jackie and I follow off to the glen. It feels nice to have space and nature around us, fresh air and calmness. We move out of the glen and back to my room, pure spangled that night as the glen has dodgy things going on in the night. There are stories of girls lying back and sucking and fucking line-ups on boys/men in the glen at night – not my kind of game.

How I learned to skin up

I am in my room and the door goes. "Hello Jackie," I say. "Hi," she replies. We get down to the business of smoking a joint when Jackie who I think has PMT and is also having boyfriend trouble says, "I am fed up of rolling joints for you! What you gonna do if I'm not around?" "I don't know," I reply, "have a bong!"

"Look," she continues as she shows me how to roll a joint which we then smoke. I try and fail miserably.

"Here," she says as she puts some dope fags and Rizla on my desk. "I have to go away for a few days, when I come back I want you to roll me a joint, OK?" She bids her farewell and then takes off with my bong. I have no choice but to learn; it takes all night but the desire to smoke a joint is strong. I am proud of my third attempt – still a crisp bag to smoke but at least it smokes and doesn't fall apart like the rest of them!

THE BASTARD AND ME

The bastard fancies me but really he has evil in his mind. The reason I call him 'bastard' is that there is no other fit name for a person like this, you will see why. I go to his room with Rizle. His room is dark with the curtains open only a little even though it is the day. He has blonde hair cut short with a little spike on top, he also wears glasses. He is thin and pale. His room is tidy and there are about two or three other boys about 16 years old in the room and they seem to be tidying and doing this man's bidding.

"Hi, how you both doing?" the bastard asks us. "Have a seat," he continues, motioning one of the boys to move for me.

"We're fine," says Rizle, "this is my mate Katie, she is new in the hostel."

"Hello Katie!"

"Hello!" I reply.

"I heard there was a new lass in here, so why you in here then, what's your story?"

"My dad and mum kicked me out, but they chose to kick me out into here."

"Fucking weird that eh! I'll kick you out but tell you where to go. How old are you, Katie?"

"Sixteen."

"How did you meet our Rizle here?"

"We just got talking in the hostel lobby."

"Do you fancy getting high?"

"On what?" I reply.

"I've got some amitriptyline, it's kinda like Valium, you ever taken Valium before?"

"Yes."

"Do fancy a couple of these?"

'Might as well' I thought, it might pass some time as really I had nothing else to do; also I had had vallies before and they were good, it was like getting really stoned without having to smoke. "OK then," I reply back.

"I will just give you two," the bastard says.

I take them and next thing I know is I wake up some time later. I don't know how long it is that I am out but fear takes over me straight away. I look around the room and the younger boys have gone and there is only Rizle and the bastard there. 'Maybe I have been raped' I think; I make a mental check on my body and clothes but nothing seems to be wrong, but being alone in a room full of men passed out is very dodgy. I leave immediately, making some excuse like "Oh! Is that the time?"

I get back to my room and I give myself a good check-over to make sure I have not being violated in any way. I am so angry with myself for allowing myself to be put in such a dangerous situation. Stupid bitch! Stupid cow, what were you thinking? I am scolding myself and at the same time promising not to put myself in that position again. I calm down with a sense of relief that I am OK. I have a joint and begin to relax; I am due to meet my boyfriend Laky in a couple of hours so have to pull myself together. All day though I carry the dull ache of fear in all my muscles and bones.

Then just as I am about to leave to go to Laky's the bastard stops me on the stairs.

"Hello, you feeling all right?"

"Yes I am fine!" I try to show no sign of the fear he had instilled in me.

"You are looking so beautiful, have you changed? I was wondering if you would like to come hang out with me later, we could have a smoke and get to know each other better."

"I can't actually, I am just away to meet my boyfriend," I say, thankful that I have a real reason and I will not have to lie.

"Ah! That's a shame," he responds, "if ever this boyfriend and you don't work out come and see me, maybe we could get something going."

"I think we will be fine," I say, trying to convince not only him but me as nothing was fine or stable in my life. I am in and out of abuse and danger every day. So off I go to see my boyfriend at the local snooker hall.

"Hello," I say to Jack, one of Laky's mates, he is a tough boy around town, the head of the townies gang

"Hello Katie, how you doing?"

"Ah! You know, all right," I reply. "Where's Laky?"

"I don't know," he says in a cagey manner, "maybe he is caught up with something," he continues.

"Aye, caught up in Sharon no doubt," says a lassie in the corner of the room.

"What do you mean?" I ask.

"Did you not know, doll? He's been fucking Sharon behind your back."

"I don't believe you, I don't even know you, how do you know my business?" I query.

"Word travels fast about this town."

"Here," says Jack, "have a drink, and you shut up Jess, it's not your business."

"Suit yourself," she replies and gets up and leaves.

"Do you mind if I hang about with you for a wee bit then?" I ask Jack.

"No that's fine, grab a cue, we'll have a game, I'm just waiting for someone myself."

Jack's mate comes in. He is some mad gangster type but very loyal to you if you keep on his right side, as are a lot of people in this drugs world. They are your deepest friends, but if you step one foot out of line or try to break free you are toast.

We hang about the pub for a while. I get on well with the lads and make some good contacts to get acid and speed so that I can supply it to my mates. It always amazes me how many friends you have when you've got drugs in your pocket.

I bid my farewells and head back to the hostel with no Laky. He has not turned up which has devastated me as I thought I was in love with him, but no way anybody's gonna see me break in some pub in the town, I will wait till my door is closed. I'm home if that's what you call it, I am so upset and have managed to keep it in for the walk home but no longer can I hold back the tears. PRICK! I think he said he loved me, I am so stupid to go on in this spiral, I think 'fuck him and stupid me for believing the words he said'.

So many men have said they love me. It is always a weak point with me, I get confused between sex and love. All I want is love and they keep saying they love me and then they cast me aside like a piece of rubbish. I am seen as the slut and they the stud; fuck this shit I have had enough. I know what it is all about. Last week I thought I may have been pregnant as I was late for my period. I went to him to tell him and he told me it was bullshit; my periods came a few days later. I am so fucked up! How am I going to survive? I am stupid and I can't tell the difference between love and sex. Right, NO MORE MEN. I promise to myself no more men. I will try but I hate being lonely; I just want to be loved.

There is a knock at my door.
"Who is it?" I am trying to make my face look decent.
"It's Rizle!"
"Come in," I say. I'm not really wanting to see anyone but I'm hoping for some support. I also want to know what had gone on in the bastard's room today.
"Hello Rizle, how you doing?"
"I am fine, what's up? Your face looks all red, have you been crying?"
"Yes! Laky and I broke up, not that he has even told me. He didn't turn up to meet me and I have heard he is fucking some

girl called Sharon."

"Fuck him," says Rizle, "you don't need anything like that, I just want to see you are all right."

"Yes, I'm fine. By the way what happened in bastard's room earlier?"

"Well, when you passed out he told the other boys to go and do some stuff for him. He wanted me to leave too, but I refused cos I didn't want to leave you on your own with him when you were passed out. He kept trying to get me involved in his shit, but I persuaded him that another hit of smack would do the trick. I gave him a healthy one and he passed out for a bit. The bastard and you started to come round at the same time. He was disappointed to see you leave," explains Rizle.

"Yeah I know, he came to see me later to ask if we could get it on but I told him that I had a boyfriend who I was just going to meet." At this point I pause trying to fight back the tears from earlier. I am so relieved that nothing happened to me. "What do you mean, his shit?" I say, remembering what Rizle had said earlier.

Rizle proceeds to tell me that the bastard likes to persuade young girls and boys to have sex with him using many different tactics and that he had been diagnosed with HIV. He is venomous and wants to pass the disease on to as many people as he can before he dies.

"BASTARD!" I say, "don't tell him I don't have a boyfriend, OK?"

"OK," replies Rizle.

Later that night I go out to sell some stuff and get wasted, it has been a hard day. I start to down some Buckfast with such power of speed in me. The next thing I know I have ran into that bastard who has some of his wee boys with him. Pain and hurt rages in my eyes as I shout, "You fucking bastard! You are evil and I hope you die!" I think it helps that we are in public so that he can't run at me and attack me. Although maybe he is a coward and has to be sly with his abuse and cannie stand a face to face fight with someone (even an emaciated girl like me).

I decide to phone the police the next day to tell them about what he has been doing and ask if there is a law against it. The police tell me that unless I can prove he is deliberately spreading the HIV virus then they can do nothing about it. They say that they have heard of this man but have no proof against him. I say to the police that he deals in smack and that he has little boy runners. This bastard is the one and only person I phone the police about in my life.

It has been nice meeting Rizle; let me share a few things about him with you. Rizle is kind and a gentleman. He is about six feet tall with shoulder-length greasy hair. His fingers are always dirty and he is so skinny. One night last week we were in his room. I was getting stoned on hash and Rizle was getting high on smack (I have never touched smack and Rizle never touched hash). Rizle started to tell me about the bastard and how he knew about his HIV and the games that he played. He began to tell me that when he was at school (he would have been about 15 years old) he didn't really have many friends. He was a bit of a loner and was always getting bullied. It was at this point that he met the bastard.

He was always really nice to him and would stop people from

battering him which meant that he was soon left alone. Bastard was about seven years older than Rizle. One day the bastard had invited Rizle to his place telling him that he had some good things to do. Rizle couldn't remember what exactly bastard had to do, but it sounded like fun and he was starting to trust him, after all he had stopped the other kids from beating him up. When Rizle was in this man's house he gave him some juice to drink and then went and put his arms around him. He said that he remembers feeling a quick panic and was just about to act on his gut instincts when he felt a sudden prick. The next thing that he remembers was waking up slightly kind of there but unable to move and the bastard was raping him. Rizle found out later that he did the same thing to lots of young boys. The sex was not only about sex, it was about control. He waited till he came around fully with his pants and trousers around his ankles and told them that he couldn't tell anyone about what had just happened; if he did bastard would say that Rizle was lying. He said he would also get one of his boys to say that Rizle was a gay arse-fucker and then he would really get a beating at school. Rizle was so ashamed when the bastard had physically finished with him that his spirit was broken. This really scared Rizle and he wasn't sure when or what had been taken from him, but it was if his spirit had deserted him.

Rizle was told by bastard to return the next week at the same time or he would look for him. He then left the man's house carrying his violated body and his soul broken. He went back after that out of fear and besides he had nowhere to run or hide. The next time bastard started to add smack into the mix and slowly Rizle became addicted. After that Rizle wasn't sure if he was gay or straight and by that time he had a hunger for smack.

CHAPTER 4

The bastard used to say to him, "Boy here's your medicine. Aren't I good to you?" When the smack started to take effect he would say, "See, you can trust me. I know what you need, I can help you. You just come to me if you are feeling bad."
The sex attacks had seemed to stop once Rizle became addicted. "The bastard had no interest in me in that way anymore and he acted like he had never done so." This left Rizle confused as to whether it had really happened or not.

One day he went to him shaking and asking for his medicine. The bastard told him that he couldn't keep getting it for free, it was expensive. He would find himself agreeing with him, as if he owed him something for helping him out with his growing need for smack. "I know," bastard continued, "I have a job for you." That was it, Rizle was hooked. He used to run drugs to and fro for his friends, steal anything he could get his hands on and commit robbery. Smack was his bind and now with addiction he could see no way out. Then Rizle told me that even today he is under his control. He has been in and out of jail for drug-related crimes and he can't get off of smack.

"That's awful." I try to say something that can help but feel that anything I say will be futile. "Do you want to get off smack?"
"Yes," replies Rizle.
"Can I help? Is there anything I can do to help you break free from him?"
"I need a friend," says Rizle.
"I am already your friend," I say, "and I will help. One thing that I can promise you, Rizle, is that you will never have any smack from me even if you ask."
"OK!"

There is silence for a while as I digest all the news that he has told me and maybe Rizle is digesting the fact that he has finally told someone.

Later on in my bedroom I can't stop thinking about the torment all those young souls are going through. I want to kill the bastard. There are rumours that he has to sleep with a gun under his pillow; I am not surprised.

I see these boys uptown all the time, running, stealing bags and robbing stuff from shops. I had no idea as to the evil in which they live and how they were being treated as disposable income. When one of them is banged up or dies there is always another vulnerable child who has suffered from a bad home to step in as a replacement. The bastard victimises and preys on these children; how can they break free? It is clear that Rizle is used goods. His eyes are wide open now after years with that bastard. He no longer serves a purpose. He is a liability, as he is well known by the police and looks like a junkie so he can't steal from clothes shops. All of his self-worth is slowly depleting if not already gone. 'The snake, the rat, the cat and the dog. How you gonna see them if you're living in the fog?' (ref. DMX). I have just reminded myself of my own vulnerability, my own near miss with the bastard. I wonder what Rizle really did to stop that man from raping me. I think about the total breakdown in communication between me and my family and why at 16 years old I'm all alone in a world of dangers, dangers that are becoming more apparent to me as time goes on. This hostel is a learning ground and I am scared.

Rizle and I are good mates. We are the most unlikely pair: I am a small techno-speed fiend and he is an emaciated tall junkie. We begin to hang out with each other at Rizle's room and in my flat. The plan is to try and stay away from bastard, which is really hard for Rizle as he has a room down the hall from him. We aim to get Rizle just to stay on his methadone rather than injecting. That will take away some of that bastard's control over him. I am going to make sure that we both eat properly as well. Rizle goes off to the centre to steal food and brings it back for me to cook. What feasts we are eating! We care about each other and it is a giving friendship that seems to nourish us in some way.

It does not take long before the tongues in the hostel are wagging, saying me and Rizle are shagging, because of course a man and woman can't possibly be friends, right?

I am sitting in Rizle's room on his soft chair and he is on his bed when he says, "You heard the rumours?"

"No, what rumours?" I reply.

"We are meant to be going out with each other and fucking."

"Oh really, is that so and how well is that?" I reply sarcastically.

"I reckon we should give them something more to talk about."

"What you thinking, Katie?" Rizle says with a smile appearing across his face.

I start to moan and groan and rock on the chair. "Come, join in Rizle."

He is giggling and says, "You are crazy, they will hear!"

"Aye, that's the plan, let's start the party!"

Rizle starts to jump on his bed and moan and groan and laugh out loud.

I am giving an Emmy performance by now and Rizle carries on jumping and groaning and laughing. We finish off with a big crescendo and then we die down. By now you can hear the voices of the other residents along the hall. We are trying hard not to laugh out loud.

Jackie has been away for some time while all this has been happening and, as usual, just as I am starting to think that she is never coming back, she turns up.

"Hello," she announces.

"Hello, I have missed you," I say.

"What's been happening?"

I proceed to tell her about my and Rizle's alleged affair, about Laky and how I am hungry and sick of the hostel.

Just as I finish talking and Jackie agrees with me that she is hungry as well, there is a knock at the door. It's Rizle with bad news.

He tells me that the hostel has found some needles under his window and someone told them they were his.

"Are they?" I ask.

"No they aren't, I think bastard is pissed off as I haven't used in a while and I haven't seen him in a while, he must have heard about us. His room is only two windows away from mine, I think he threw them under my window."

"What's the hostel going to do about it?"

"They said that it's very serious and that they can't risk having any needles in the place. They have given me a week to find somewhere else to stay."

"Can I not help? Tell them what's been happening?"

"No Katie, I will move. I hate living near bastard anyway."

"Well we must do something about our hunger then, you hungry Rizle?"

"Yeah, why?"

"We are all hungry, you fancy using your talents to get us all some food?"

"I will cook," says Jackie.

"I will clean. We can have a really nice meal together."

"OK," says Rizle, "what do you want?"

Jackie gives him a list and off he goes to the shops. I like the way Jackie looks after me when she is here. I have missed her as it seems like ages since I last saw her.

Rizle arrives with the booty. Jackie cooks it and we all eat like kings and queens sat around the table together.

"Why don't you leave here, Katie?" Jackie says.

"Where would I go? I don't know anywhere to stay. I have tried once but that was so bad I ended up back here."

"Where did you go?" Jackie asks me.

"To this woman called Jess. She stays in Dunfress with her husband who kicks her face in, so she kicked him out and I had the spare room. I looked after her baby when she was working."

"What went wrong?" asks Jackie.

"Her husband came back. One day I came home to find her alone, all the pictures were smashed and she had a fat lip and a bruised face. Once I saw him drag her across the shingle and smack her so I squared up to him."

"Good for you," says Jackie, "he sounds like a fucking bastard."

"Yeah and the next time I come home and he has moved in again and my bags are packed as I am a threat to him. I am removed and back to the hostel I go."

"It won't be like that at a friend I know in Sheckledone."

"That's a nice offer, I will think about it. I have had an offer off one of the girls in here to stay with her. She is moving to Abbey View and I have been accepted on the Nursery Nurse course in Dunfress."

"Well the offer's there," says Jackie.

"Thanks Jackie, I may well need it. Where you gonna go, Rizle?"

"I don't know, I will look in town."

We finish our meal and chill out. Jackie and I start getting on with rolling joints.

"I am impressed you have learned well," she admires as we smoke.

"Thanks for the push," I say.

A week later and I have been speaking to my friend Lexus, she is the girl who has offered me a place to stay in Abbey View. I have been accepted at college to do Nursery Nursing but I am a bit worried about my health. It's tough though, I must go on and try to qualify in something I like in order to eventually earn a wage and get a home of my own.

Rizle has moved into town so I decide I will go and see him and tell him of my new address.

"Hello, how are you Rizle?"

"Ah not bad, you know nothing changes much."

I go into his room that he is renting which is in the attic of an old town house.

The room is smelly because of the overflowing ashtrays but I don't mind though.

As we sit down Rizle asks me if I want a cup of tea.

"Yes please."

He gets up to go to and wash a cup which is stained with tea and has fag ash in it. He looks sad again and I can see evidence all around him chasing smack.

"I've got some news," I say.

"Yeah what's that?" asks Rizle.

"I have been accepted on a college course in Dunfress." I tell him what the course involves and about me moving to my mate Lexus's hoose.

"When you moving? I have some news as well," he says.

"What's your news?" I ask him.

"I am moving in a week's time. I am going to jail!"

"Why?"

"I was caught nicking some stuff from the town and I got away with a lot, so they decided it was time I visited jail again. I will be in for three months, will you come visit me?"

"I will try but I can't promise as I will be at college and I don't have a lot of money. I will defo write to you though."

"That will be nice. I will look forward to it."

We chill for the afternoon chatting to one another. Then I have to go and get ready to move. We bid our farewells. The end of my time in the hostel is nigh and I am pretty excited to be going off on my own; I have a college course and a new home. I am quietly confident.

The week has passed really fast and I am moving today. A staff member at the hostel and Lexus help me to move.

I arrive at Lexus's on the Friday night. I have been at college for a week now and I am lucky enough to attend a placement in a primary school just along from my house. I will be going there three days a week and to college for the other two days.

However, all is not well with Lexus today.

"Hello Katie."

"Hi, how are you? Have you had a good day?"

"No, I have been to see Dillon. My mum's a fucking arsehole, she always treats him like he is hers." Her mum looks after her son as she gave him to her because she couldn't cope with a child all the time in the house.

"I'm sorry to hear that."

"I have sorted some things in the cupboard for you. Here's a space where you can put your food and stuff and this is your room." The room is fine with a single bed in it. Some of her stuff is still in my new room, but it's not a problem as it is a temporary arrangement.

After settling in I say to Lexus, "Do you want a tea?"

"Have you bought any tea bags?"

"Not yet."

"Well you can't just use mine!"

I think that her reaction to my answer is very weird but I have to keep this place or I am in shit.

"OK I will just nip to the shop and get some stuff, do you want anything?"

"Yeah! Some Dorchester cigs and Rizla please."

I get back to the house and make the tea.

"Would it be possible for me to have a key to come and go?" I ask Lexus.

"No, I won't give you a key, you will have to work around me."

"What about when I am at college?" I question.

"We will work something out."

I'm starting to get worried. This is not as nice as I thought it would be.

That night I go to visit a couple of friends that I have made in the local area. We get the spats knives out and we start having spats. The more stoned I get, the more I start to tell my new friends about my situation. They find my situation as strange as I do. They tell me to see what the week brings and to keep in touch with them.

Monday comes and I don't have to get up early as my placement is only five minutes away. Suddenly there is a loud bang on the door.

"What's wrong?" I say to Lexus.

"You're oversleeping!"

"No it's all right, my placement's just down the road."

"Yeah but I have to leave at half eight and so do you, as you can't lock the door without the key. I will be back at 6:00 p.m."

"What?" I ask, stunned. "You want me to stand in the street for half an hour? Why can't you give me the spare key? I am paying you money, do I not get any freedom of entry? I'm not gonna do anything!"

"You could stay in all day then you don't need to lock the door, or you can leave altogether," is her response.

So here I am, cold and hungry with 30 minutes to waste. I'm in a place where nutters and junkies live and who sleep in unless it is Giro day. What a strange girl Lexus is. My stomach is in pain, as I don't have any money for anything to eat. I have had no time to prepare for college today.

I go to my placement and try my best to function properly today, but it's very hard when you are hungry. I don't know what is going on in my stomach, but it is not good. The next day I choose to stay in.

I stay in bed as Lexus leaves in the morning and I am unable to leave the house as I'm not allowed the spare key. Maybe I can leave the door unlocked and come and go as I please, but that would too risky in this part of town (the house will probably be robbed if I do that). I decide to risk it anyway; I go round to my friend's place in the afternoon. I share my worries with my friend and she tells me about a spare room that she knows about. The flat belongs to one of our mate's brothers in Sheckledone. It is further away from college, but never mind it's better than where I am at the moment. It transpires that I will be able to move into the flat in a month's time. I don't know how much more of this restricted madness I can take.

The next day I receive a letter from Rizle. He tells me that he is OK and that he will be out very shortly. He wants me to visit him and has put £20 in with the letter and tells me to buy a new pair of jeans for myself with it. He has also drawn a map of the prison for me. Unbeknown to me 'buy a new pair of jeans' translates into 'buy me some jelly eggs and smuggle them into the jail'. Ignorance is bliss sometimes. When he gets out of jail I go and see him and he asks me why I didn't visit him and where the money is that he sent me. I show him my new jeans and he starts to laugh and calls me a silly bugger.

When I arrive home that evening Lexus tells me that I have to leave tomorrow and that I should go and stay with one of my other friends.

CHAPTER 5

The Limpet and Other Fabulous Boyfriends

I will start this chapter by telling you about Daniel. He is a tall man who is 12 years older than me (I am 16). He is good-looking, with a strong jawline and shoulder-length wavy black hair and big hands. I like big hands.

We met in a club called Landers's. I was dealing speed there; I used to deal to all the women customers as they trusted me. My shit was uncut and I gave good deals. This particular night I had taken five Ecstasys and a bag of speed; I am dancing and enjoying myself when I suddenly start to come up. I feel the urge to throw up so I make my way to the fire exit and open both of the doors.

After throwing up I close the doors and carry on dancing. The bouncers are on to me in the club, but I always stash my gear really well so when they search me they never find anything. I am on the stairs being searched when Daniel comes around the corner. He is well known to the bouncers and he says that he knows me and that I'm cool, so they let me go. Later that night some of my mates and I go to Daniel's house. We party; I am so E'd up that my jaw is bouncing up and down, as if I am freezing. This is known as jittery jaw. Most of the people from the party start to leave, but I am homeless so I really have nowhere in particular to go. I decide to hang around at Daniel's house but I don't tell him this though, I just act cool. He tells me that he has a spare room and I'm welcome to use it to crash for the night. I accept the offer with relief, and finally, after hours of getting stoned, I crash in his spare room.

The next morning I say I have some shit to sort out and I have to go. I thank him for letting me stay and walk to the door to leave. As I start to leave, Daniel asks, "What you doing tonight?"

"I don't have too many plans, why what are you thinking?"

"Well my house will be free for the weekend, if you want to stay and hang out you can use the spare room."

"That would be excellent!" I say. "I will go and sort some business out and then if I come back at around six is that OK?"

"Yeah that's fine, maybe we can get a carry out."

"Yeah, that's cool."

I make my way into town, do some deals and sell some dope. I've got enough cash now to go and hang out with Daniel.

"How you doing?" I say as I get to his door.

"I am cool, just chilling. Are you coming in?"

"Yeah."

After we smoke a few joints he brings out some white powder which looks like speed. "Have you ever tried coke before?"

"No, but I don't mind trying."

"Here, snort a few lines, one up each nostril." He watches me as the lines of white powder disappear up my nostrils.

"How you feeling?" he asks me.

"Warm n' cosy," I reply.

"How about having some E's with me as well? I've got some left over from last night."

"Yeah, that's a good idea," and I take an E.

"I really like you, you are so beautiful. How did you end up leaving home?"

"My stepfather and I didn't get on. He was always calling me a bitch and a bastard; I had had enough of his shit. So it all blew up one day and I was kicked out."

"What did your mum do about it?"

"She supported him, saying I should stop reacting, I should walk away and just ignore him. It's bullshit anyway, I don't want to talk about that. What's going on at the weekend? Any raves?"

"Yeah there's the Rez. You want to come with me?"

"What, go together?" I ask.

"Yeah, why not, we could have some fun, you could stay here for a wee while if that suits you better."

"What, here with you?"

"Well, I've got the spare room. I can't have a beautiful woman like you running about the streets alone, who knows what will happen? I care, even if your family doesn't."

I feel wanted at that moment and he called me a woman. I am so happy somebody finally realises that I am a woman and not a child.

"Do you want another line of coke?" Daniel asks.

"Yeah that would be nice, I'll roll a joint."

"How's the E doing?" Daniel asks as he is lining up some more coke to snort. "Well good. I feel very warm and cosy."

"Here, try this." He gently smoothes some coke over my lips and gums. "Feels good doesn't it?"

"Wow, my lips feel really numb."

His lips touch mine and we begin to kiss. Now my head is whirling around and around in a pleasurable daze. I am full of emotions and warm all over. The E which I took is rushing through all of my body, and the kiss feels divine. Who would imagine, me 16 and this man finds me attractive. I feel like a woman. I can feel his hands on my breasts, wherever they go the E and coke follows, accentuating the feelings. I feel my pussy getting wet with excitement and it's as if he reads my body, his big hand makes its way to my pussy. I let him undress me with ease, he slips his fingers into my wet pussy and starts to move them inside me. I start to moan, I have lost control of my body and I have given it to him. He motions to me to feel him. I take hold of his hard penis and start moving my hand up and down it; he pulls gently away and makes another line of coke.

"Let me show you something," he says, as he lays me back and spreads my legs, letting the cool air circulate around my undulating pussy. He puts some coke on his hand and places it on my clit; the feeling is bizarre, I have never felt this before. He then brings his face down and starts to lick my clit, spreading the coke everywhere. I am not sure of all these feelings, I have never felt like this before, his tongue deep inside me, all around me and the weird sensation of the coke on my pussy. He stands up in front of me and his big hard dick is right in front of me, he is telling me to suck. I am not sure what I want, but all these feelings are rushing around my body. I sink his hard penis inside my mouth, till it is deep in my throat. He starts to move it in and out of my mouth while he moans and groans with pleasure. I am pleased I can please him, so I suck with more vigour, like I am eating it all up. Then he pulls away. I lie back on the sofa and he leans into me and I feel him enter my wet pussy, he pushes up hard inside me. He feels so big and I am so tight, the drugs rush to the top of my head and I feel like my head is going to blow open at the top. He starts to get faster and harder, he uses longer strokes and I can feel my nipples get so hard. He is fucking me now and I don't know how much more I can take, but it feels so good. I am fucking him; we are fucking, yes hard and strong and then he lulls. I wonder what is going on, my pussy now is dripping wet and he pulls out from me. I wonder why he has stopped.

"What's wrong?" I say.
"Nothing!" he replies. "I have just come. Wasn't that nice, baby?

Do you want another line of coke?"
We take coke all weekend and fuck all weekend. He tells me
that he loves me and I think I love him too. Finally some good
luck in my life, just when I was beginning to think it was all shit.
I am glad I don't live at home. I will live here with Daniel, as he
loves me. We love each other; I have never felt like this before.

I wake up the next afternoon to the smell of bacon cooking, wow
this is great! I am gonna love living here.
"I have to go out," says Daniel. "Why don't you stay in and
watch some TV? I have some business to take care of."
"OK, thanks." I have nothing else to do and I'm feeling pretty
much on a comedown. Daniel comes into the room with a bacon
sandwich and a joint.
"Here you are. Enjoy your day, I will be back later!"
"See you later!"

He comes back later that day with his cousin and introduces me
to him.
"Hello Katie! Did you have a nice day?"
"Yeah, I slept for most of it, I was pretty tired."
"Hello," I say to his cousin.
"Oh sorry, this is Jamie. We have been hanging out together
today, thought you'd like to meet some of my family."
"Nice to meet you," he says.
"Hey Daniel, you got them E's?" asks Jamie.
"Yeah, I'll just get them."
"So, I hear you will be staying with Daniel for a while, yeah?"
"Yeah, we have been hanging out with each other for a while.
Are you coming to the Rez at the weekend?"
"Yeah I will be there; I will probably come in the car with you."

"How's about we get a Chinese?" suggests Daniel.

"Good idea," Jamie and I reply.

We eat the Chinese and Jamie pops out to get a bottle of Buckfast. Daniel suggests that we take some E's. We all agree and take two E's each. Ah, it's that E feeling again, I start to come up as we all watch a movie. I go to the toilet and when I come back Jamie says he has to go out for a while, maybe he'll catch up with us tomorrow. We say our goodbyes.

"Do you want a drink?" I say to Daniel. "Yeah, some water would be nice." I go to the kitchen to fetch some water, and when I come back Daniel has some lines of coke set up for us. "You want some?" he asks.

"Yeah." We have a few lines and I need to go to the toilet again, as I have a quick come-up. I come back into the room and Daniel has taken his trousers off. He is sitting there with this hard erect penis. I am unnerved by this, and was hoping to just chill and talk, but my thoughts are interrupted by him saying, "Come and sit on my hard dick, girl, you know you like it!"

He is holding his hand out to me. He turns me around so as I am facing away from him and he slips my trousers and pants down and guides me to sit down on his penis. My pussy is sore from last night, but I sit on him, my mind is trying to complain, but my body is being convinced. "You know I love you," he says, "you know I want you around. Let's go to the bedroom, I want to fuck you."

He guides me to his bedroom. We are fucking again, and having lines of coke again and again. I feel this sharp pain in my arse, I think maybe it's his finger in me and that he has a sharp nail.

When we finish I try to hold my bowels in, but it's no use, I make an excuse and go to the toilet. The next thing I know I am waking up from lying on the bathroom floor; there is blood all over the floor and the room stinks of shit. Daniel has been trying to wake me up. He says that I have been there for hours.

"What happened?"

"I don't know," he says looking really worried. We both decide to call a doctor to make sure that I'm all right. The next day things have changed between Daniel and me. He isn't complimenting me anymore and he appears to be distant with a strange look in his eyes. He tells me that he has received a phone call from his wife and that he wants to give it another try with her again. He says I am welcome to use the spare room for a week, and that we can now only be friends. My world suddenly shatters. I am going to be homeless again, and he has a wife. This is news to me; I'm not in a position to complain as I will need to use the spare room for a week to get my shit together. I am in a daze and this just confirms to me that life is shit and that I am worthless baggage easily used then discarded.

A couple of days have passed now and Daniel hasn't been here at all, but I know that he will be here so maybe we can talk? He arrives at about six o'clock but he is with his cousin so talking to him is going to be impossible tonight. Very soon the drink and drugs come out again.

"Hello Katie, how's it going?" asks Jamie.

"Fine," I reply. 'Well, as fine as it things can be' I think to myself. It won't be long till I am on the streets again.

"Here have some coke, it's good stuff."

"OK!" I reply. I don't care any longer, I feel dead inside.

CHAPTER 5

"Have some Buckfast as well and I will put some music on."
Jamie goes over to the stereo and puts some techno on. I drink
the Buckfast and start to enjoy the feeling of complete numbness
that the drink and drugs give me. They give me a break from
reality.

"Do you want some E's?" Daniel asks. "It might cheer you up."

"OK!"

I have now left the building so to speak, my mind is entering
that space where sadness is disguised as not caring, not feeling.
"I need to go lie down," I say. "I'll help you get to your bed,"
volunteers Jamie.

"OK," I reply, not really registering anything.

I am not sure where I am. I must have blacked out, I am slowly
coming round and I can feel that someone's inside me. Who is
it? All my senses slowly come back and I realise Jamie is fucking
me. He seems to be having a rare old time, he is smiling and
fucking. Did I ask for this? Do I want this? The E and the coke
that I have taken are going around my body; shall I make a sign?
Call 'rape' or just go with it? It will be over soon – well, if he
hasn't taken speed. Oh! But he has been drinking Buckfast. Fuck
it, I will fuck the bastard.

"You want to fuck?" I say. "I'll fuck you till your dick falls off,
fucker!" I start fucking him till my pussy tears and is bleeding. I
am in and out of consciousness and am angry. I want to kill him
by fucking him to death, wipe that smile right off his face. I pass
out again and when I wake up he seems to be finished with me
and I reach for the Buckfast and take a good swally. I want to be
unconscious again; I feel like shit. I pass out and leave the house
the next day.

I have a message from Daniel. He wants to see me. I am all excited by the thought that he wants me again. When I arrive he tells me that he is sorry about finishing with me, and that he wants to make it up to me by taking me out into Edinburgh for the night. I'm so happy and maybe a night out together is what we need. We are in the car together and on our way to Edinburgh.

"Where are we going?" I ask.

"We are going to a club called Carlton for a techno night," he replies.

I start to take a few E's then some speed and an acid tab. My mind is bending as we arrive at the club. Daniel seems to know a lot of people there and I don't know anyone. We walk through the club hallway which is painted white and has camy nets hanging from the ceiling. At the end of the hall are some stairs which lead to the chill-out room on my left, and to the right is a door which leads on to the dance floor. I try and stay close to Daniel while we are dancing. He then leans over to me and says in my ear, "I gotta go and do something, will be back soon," and with that said he disappears. Just then I feel a sharp pain in my stomach and I rush to the toilet. As I enter the toilets, there is a queue. I am trying to be cool; I am alone in this club, I feel like Mrs No-Pals. There is toilet paper all over the floor; I am hoping there is some in the fucking toilet. I enter the cubicle and the white walls and toilet are framed by the red brick floor. It seems to be moving away from me and the pain takes over, and I finally let up what has been trying to come out for ten minutes now. I am being sick so badly that the pain is ripping through my stomach, I see blood in the toilet and I start to become scared for my life. I am about six stone and puking blood. Where is Daniel? I go and look for him as soon as I can but I can't find him anywhere.

People ask me if I am OK; I must look freaked. Everyone around seems to be E'd up. They are chewing imaginary gum, their faces are bending and they are covered with ultraviolet paints. Everyone looks evil and I am all alone, I am sick and vulnerable but if anyone asks I am fine; no problems. Fuck, where is he? The room is spinning; I am scared and I don't know how to get back to Fife. Someone tells me that Daniel is at their house, and if I want to go and rest and see him they will take me. When I get there Daniel is chillin', having a smoke. 'Great', I think to myself, 'thanks for your friendship'. Tonight was a disaster, and I am in pain, but I have to wait till he is ready to take me back to Fife, but why? I don't know! I have nowhere to live, but at least I know how to scam a survival there.

With friends like these

I have been floating around like a bad smell. I have been living in and out of houses, and on the streets, robbing shops for food and clothes. I keep selling small amounts of drugs to try and get some money. Sometimes I sleep in the ruins of the castle in the glen or on hard stairwells. Otherwise I party for days, even weeks, and just wait until I pass out somewhere. It's amazing how you can go to the shopping centre with no money in your pocket and leave with a new jumper, food in your belly, and some smokes.

I see Lewis.
"How's it goin' Katie?"
"Well, you know, same old shit, just a different day!"
"You got any gear?"
"Yeah I got a power of shit, why, you got some plans?"
"Yeah, let's take it to my ma's, she's away for the weekend, you

can sleep there if you want."

"Cool, I will need to get to my stash."

"Cool, I will meet you at the bus station at 6:00 p.m."

Six o'clock rolls around and Lewis is waiting for me at the bus station.

"All right? What's going down, babes?"

"Not a lot, are we off to your house then?"

"Yeah sure."

We get to his house and he breaks open the vodka.

Time passes and he's heavy with the come-ons.

"Hey Katie!" he says in a wasted voice.

"What?"

"Do you, or could you fancy me?"

"Me? Na Lewis, you are a mate, ain't no fancying going on."

We keep on drinking. Ah fuck, not again! I have blacked out; I wake up and Lewis is fucking me. For fuck's sake, is it not possible to rest anywhere without people always fucking with you? Will I punch him? No, I get to stay here for the weekend, it's warm, there's food, and a bed. Ah fuck it, smug bastard; I hope his dick falls off. When he's finished I can have a bath and eat. Lewis seems to be a bit scared about what he has just done, but it was short and it's over now.

"You fucking sly bastard! Fucking me when I am passed out."

"No, you wanted it, you asked for it."

"What, in my sleep, fucker? Anyway there's one, call it rent."

And with that I get some grub and run myself a bath.

Later on we take some speed and drink a bottle of Buckfast before we head off to a mate's house in town. There's no way that I'm going to sleep; I will be on E and speed all night, I don't fancy any more fucking. The night passes and we are talking really fast about important shit; I stress the shit part. We meet up with Mark, Dillon and Sharon.

"What you up to tonight?" I ask Sharon.

"We're gonna take the car to Kirkcaldy to a rave, you fancy coming?"

"Yeah I've got fuck all else happening, you coming Lewis?"

"Na, I'm gonna go home to bed before my mum comes back. See ya later!"

"Bye!" I say, wishing I could go somewhere and rest. I'm only awake because of the amount of drugs holding me up. In the last three days I have had two grams of speed, three E's, a bottle of vodka, a bottle of Buckfast and have smoked large amounts of grass.

I decide to take another E and a wee bit more speed, you know, to keep me awake. We dance all night at the rave.

"Do you fancy an acid, Katie?" Sharon asks me.

"Yeah, why not?" I reply but as soon as I start to come up, I realise I have made a big mistake. I am fucking out my head; I am still dancing when the rave finishes in the morning.

"I am going to stay at Dillon's house, Katie. You gonna be all right from here?"

"I don't know how to get home," I say with paranoia ripping through my brain.

"I'll get someone to give you a lift. Mark can't as he is working tomorrow."

"Thanks that would be good."

"Here, I want you to meet Bill and Jason, they are my mates."

"Hi, how you doing?" I say, shaking their hands.

"We are fine. Sharon says you need a lift."

"Yeah I do, are you going to Dunfress?"

"Yeah we've got a flat there."
 I get into their car and we go off to Dunfress.

The car is a black Ford Escort. As I step inside I can smell the stale smoke and beer; I move the roaches and beer cans that are on the floor of the car with my feet. I sit in the back of the car feeling happy that soon I will be near to the streets that I know.
"Where you wanting to be dropped off?" asks Bill.
"Just at the bus station please."
"Where do you live?"
"Well here, there, everywhere."
"Do you have anywhere to go?"
"I'm kinda in between houses."
"We're not going to be going straight to sleep. You could come back for a smoke, hang out at ours for a while," Jason says.
"Cool, thanks." A slight reprieve from the streets, but where am I gonna sleep? I know that I will pass out at some point, but not in a house with men, as it is not safe. I know of a disused building off the glen. I will have a J and a cup of tea, warm up a bit and then make my way to the old cold buildings. We arrive at their flat and make our way up the one flight of stairs to the front door. Bill opens the door and lets me in.
"Come in, make yourself at home." He quickly clears the sofa of its rubbish.
"Thanks," I say. The wallpaper is yellow with smoke; the table just in front of the sofa is covered with beer cans, some of which have been used as ashtrays. There is a strong smell – a mixture of sweaty socks, stale smoke and beer. I'm sure I can smell a dog. Bill starts to try and clean the small living room. He then turns on the bar fire and switches the stereo on.

"Do you want a tea?" Jason asks.

"Yes, that would be nice, thanks."

"Have a seat," says Bill motioning to the sofa, "I'm going to help Jason with the tea."

"OK." I sit down and try to adjust to the airless living room. I don't feel 100% safe, but I am warm and not out on the streets. I hear a scraping sound coming from the room next door.

Jason comes in and opens the door. "This is Windsun."

"What kinda dog is he?"

"He's a bull terrier. Do you want sugar in your tea?"

"Yes, just one." Jason disappears into the kitchen again, and I can hear them talking; I start to make friends with Windsun.

Jason brings my tea and takes a seat next to me; I notice that Bill is locking the front door and I hear three locks being shut. I follow him with my gaze as he goes to the room that Windsun was in. He leaves the door open a bit. Through the open door I can see that he is puffing up the pillows and turning back the covers on the bed. The atmosphere starts to change and I try to cause a distraction.

"This is nice tea, thanks Jason."

"That's all right, glad you like it."

"I'll make a joint yeah, and then I better be off."

"Where you gonna go? You don't have to leave so soon, make yourself comfy."

Bill comes back into the room and sits down next to me on my left hand side. They both get closer to me; Bill puts his hand on my leg and starts to stroke it.

"Thanks for the lift home, the tea is lovely, but I've got a lot to do today so I must leave."

"Don't be silly, we're cool, just chill," says Bill.

Windsun is now on my lap and is turning around and barking at Jason, then at Bill, then Jason, then Bill. The atmosphere goes crazy and alarm bells in my head start to go off, the voice in my head that has saved me before is screaming 'GET OUT NOW!! GET OUT NOW!!' I pull myself up with the little energy I have left and go to the door. I start unlocking the door; Windsun is in between me and the boys, barking at them.

"What's up, why are you going crazy? We're not gonna do anything."

"I just need to go," I say.

"You have nowhere to go Katie, why not stay?" says Jason.

"I just need to open this lock, I am trapped, let me out."

Finally I manage to get the last lock open and run. I am running for my existence. When I am far enough away I stop. My chest is hurting and I am scared and very confused. It is five in the morning and I have nowhere to go. I feel hollow, cold and hungry. I have been trying to ignore my hunger pains for three days now.

Seems it's easier to get drugs than food and shelter in this life. So in a crazy, drugged-out, hungry daze I just walk, nowhere to rest. Before I know it I am at Daniel's house; I knock on the door and he comes to the door.

"Daniel, can you help me?"

"No, you can't come in here, Katie, I'm busy," he replies.

I am used to this answer by now; I'm used goods now, no longer beautiful, no longer desirable. I am hollow and sick. I walk away and look back at his house; it looks cold and unwelcoming in the cool blue of the morning. I cross the road and I freeze on the spot. I don't seem to have anything left in me to even move and I have nowhere to go. I notice that the traffic lights seem to always be at red, red, red, red; a white car comes by again and again. I am sure I see George in the car, the fact that this may be a hallucination doesn't occur to me. I pick up a brick and throw it at the car. I am still stuck to the spot when I hear a policeman say to me, "Are you all right?"

I cannot answer, I am still frozen to the spot, be it from fear, hunger, drugs or the cold I am not sure, but I can't move.
"Come on young lady, you need to come with us. Do you realise you just threw a brick through the window of this man's car?"
"Sorry," I say.
"Come on, I will help you in the van, and we will go to the station."
There are some guys in the van; one of them has a bag of bread rolls with him. They say something to me, but I can't speak. Paranoia is ripping through my mind. I think that this is a set-up; they are pretending to be the police and they are really going to kill me. I secretly hope that there's no way a guy with bread rolls in his hands would kill me.

We get to the station and the policeman gets me out of the van.
"Why did you do it? You could have caused a bad accident," the copper asks me.
"I don't know," I say.
"What's going on inside your head?" the other policeman asks me.
They start to empty all my possessions out of my pockets and take my fingerprints. They then put me into a cell and leave me there for three days.
I am bouncing off the walls, coming down off all the drugs that

I have taken. I'm sure that they are going to kill me. They give me some salty soup which I decide to use to paint a mural on my cell walls; it helps to pass some time. My hair was braided when I first arrived here, but now I look like Crystal Tipps. At the beginning of my stay the cell walls were cream in colour; there is a mattress which is as thin as a matchbox in one corner of the room and a coarse blanket sits on a wee shelf below a small window. The floor is made from concrete and is freezing cold underfoot. However, when I leave the walls are a vegetable colour and the floor is covered with a thin layer of my hair as I have pulled all my braids and curbigrips out through sheer frustration. I stash some of the curbigrips under the mattress so the next occupant can make use of them.

At last I am set free into a life of unsure nothings; they didn't kill me after all and life carries on as usual.

Ten Men

Sharon and I meet up a couple of weeks later. I decide not to tell her about what happened between, Bill, Jason and me. Dillon is a thing of the past as well.

"All right chavy?" I call to Sharon.

"Yeah, all good. What you up to, Katie?"

"Well I'm just doing some business and trying to find a home. What you been up to?"

"I was thinking of going to Glasgow. I met a sexy guy called Mich and he has invited me to his house party. Do you fancy coming? I could do with someone to come with me. You know, to chum me."

"Ah! Denny ken am a bit skint!"

"I'll pay," Sharon says.

"I can't pay you back, so it will have to be your treat!"

"OK! You're on. Meet at my house on Saturday; we can get ready and then get a bus through to Glasgow, yeah?"

"OK, see you on Saturday, bye."

We arrive in Glasgow and meet up with Mich. Now personally I think this guy is a plucky casual prick, but each to their own. He takes us to all the designer shops in Glasgow; me homeless with no money and Sharon a single mother who is on a hairdressing apprenticeship. This is the first sign that he has a high opinion of himself, and no fucking sense about other people's situations. I am followed around all the shops that I go into, as all the security staff think I am going to shoplift due to my emaciated and poor-looking appearance. My stomach is in pain and I have no patience for their bullshit, I don't want to be here, but fuck it, I have nowhere else to go, so here we go!

We arrive at Frankie's, Mich's friend's house.

"All right Mich, how's it going?"

"It's fine. Just been shopping up town, this is Sharon and her mate Katie."

"All right ladies, come on in," says Frankie.

As we walk into the house a strong smell of aftershave hits us, Frankie has just showered. He shows us to the room on the right of the door. "Here, you girls get a seat, you want a drink?"

"Yeah, you got any orange juice?" Sharon asks.

"What about you, Katie?"

"Just some water please," I say.

"Frankie, do you mind if I we have wee shower before we go out?" asks Sharon.

"Yeah that's fine."

Sharon and I take a shower and get ready to go out to the club.

We all leave together and meet up with a large group of Frankie and Mich's mates in Hanger Thirteen. The club is really busy and everyone there is wearing designer clothes. I immediately lose track of Sharon as she is following Mich around like he is a god, her behaviour inflating his already large ego. I start to feel a sharp pain in my stomach together with feelings of being under-dressed and poor. However, these feelings begin to pass, as the E that I have taken starts to take effect.

"Are you having fun?" Mich asks me.

"Yeah I'm just enjoying a wee dance, and you, how you doing?"

"I'm great; do you and Sharon fancy coming back to Frankie's for a smoke after the club?"

"I am just gonna follow what Sharon wants to do tonight, so if she goes around to your house then I will join her. Catch up with you at the end of the night, yeah?"

"OK, see you then."

I can't really communicate with anyone; I feel weird being here. I am in a lot of pain and everyone seems weird to me. I am always scared that people are judging me, so I just dance the night away. I feel so weak, but as usual I go on and lose myself in the music.

"Katie, the club's nearly over, we're gonna go to Frankie's, OK?" says Sharon.

We get to Frankie's. There is Sharon and me, with ten guys including Frankie and Mich. We are all getting stoned.

"Shall we have some jellies?" asks Mich.

There is a chorus of "Pass one over" from the guys.

"What about you girls?" Mich says.

"Yeah, I will have one," says Sharon.

"No, I'm all right thanks," I say. I know that if I take any jellies I will be out for the count. It doesn't take Sharon long to fall asleep on the chair next to me. The jelly has knocked her out. Suddenly the atmosphere begins to change; the hairs are standing up on the back of my neck, and a chill is hitting my bones. I shudder and I look around the room to take stock of what is happening. Mich is winking at me from the seat next to me; I carry out a slow sweeping look around the room, from left to right. To my horror I can see all the guys holding their hands just above their groins, as if they are holding a person and pretending to fuck them and then passing them over to their friend with him doing the same. They all start to get into a frenzy and their laughter starts to build up together with their sexual excitement. They keep looking at me and smiling and laughing, nodding their heads as they do the motion again.

"Stop it guys, just cool down. It's getting a bit silly now!" Frankie says to them all as he looks at me.

"Look! If you're not in with us, fuck off and go to bed, but put your music on, it could get a bit noisy," says this ugly-looking bastard from across the other side of the room.

I am frantically shaking Sharon.

"Wake up Sharon, wake up now Sharon!" I am begging her.

"What? I'm chilling," comes the sleepy response.

I grab hold of her face and hold it up, forcing her to open her eyes.

"You come with me now, or you can fucking stay here with these hungry bastards, I am leaving now."

The look in Frankie's eyes is enough to tell us that we are in immediate danger.

"I'm coming with you," Sharon says with real urgency in her

voice.

"Please open the door," I say to Frankie.

"Oh come on girls, stay here and play with us, we will have some fun!" the ugly bastard is saying.

"Fuck off and play with yourselves," I yell to him as we clear off through the door, "thanks Frankie."

On the bus on the way home I curse Sharon for getting me into that situation but at the same time I am also glad that I was there for her sake.

CHAPTER 6

Product of a Robbery

When I arrive in Farvo I am homeless and have nothing; I am surviving on parties alone. My mate Jackie tells me of someone called Rose in Farvo who has a room for rent. I go and see the woman whose room it is and she agrees that I can stay there. This makes me really happy as it's nice to have my own room again. My room is next to the front door, which is great as we didn't have much in common and I am always out. My bed is pretty old and used and there seems to be a musty, mouldy smell in the room. The wallpaper is peeling away from the corners of the walls because of the damp, but nevertheless it is somewhere to lay my head, it's home for now.

I am really into techno music and clubs. Rose likes rock and heavy metal and enjoys drinking in pubs. I think to myself that this could be a fresh start; it's Saturday night and I have a bed to come hame te; hame – what a barry concept. Jackie calls on me and I am so excited to open the door of my new hame, well it is my hame for the foreseeable future anyway. Jackie wants to introduce me to some Farvo folks so I bid my landlady goodbye and am off to party. We arrive at Marley's hoose; Jackie just pushes the door open.

"Alreet chavy, fancy meeting you here!" Jackie says.

"Come in and let me introduce you to Marley."

"Katie, this is Marley."

"Alreet, how's it going? Welcome to Farvo! I heard you're staying doun the road near the rock chick's hoose."

"Yeah, do you ken her like?"

"Na, no' much, just heard she's a bit of a drunk like," says Marley.

"I've got a flat coming up just behind here but it's another week before I can get in it, I need to gan doon View and sort it oot."

"Who is the little boy?"

"He is my son, his name is Jason."

"That's a lovely name."

"Thanks! Are you coming to the rave later in Cowden?" Marley asks me.

"Yeah we've got a ride like."

"Now Katie, we all have a question that any newcomer to Farvo must answer." Marley leads me into the smoky living room which is full of people and promptly starts to introduce me to them all.

"Here everyone, this is Katie. Katie this is Busby, Alli, Samo, Paul and Graham. Well anyway, back to the question!" Marley says.

I was hoping she had forgotten all about it.

"Do you want to be weaned on Buckfast or Thunderbird?" Marley asks me.

I look confused and stare over to Jackie who has a big smile on her face.

I choose Buckfast of course.

"Yeah, good choice," says Busby. He is a small man who is in his 30s, but looks much older as he is well worn. His face is covered with acne and he is wearing a dark blue denim jacket, a pair of old jeans and a T-shirt.

"Here, have a wee drink," he says passing me the Buckfast. I soon make friends with everyone, as I always have E's, acid and speed on me. My friend Jackie is well respected too, so that helps me as well. We all leave for the rave.

"Hey do you fancy dancing at the rave for us Katie?" asks Jackie.

"What do you mean?"

"Well I do some dancing on the stage, it's cool."

"OK that will be fine but I will have to wait till I come up on my E."

"Yeah and we can have a wee sniff of poppers then we're gony be flying," laughs Jackie.

When we get to the rave I can see two tables in the middle of the dance floor which are straight opposite the stage. Jackie and I get up on to them and start to dance. Before long we have synchronized and the crowd is also starting to synchronize with us and before long I am as high as I can possibly be. I have complete power over thousands of people and all I can see are people dancing and a sea of hands. What a rush! My God this is good! Then I feel a tap on my shoulder.

"Follow me," Jackie says. I follow her into a car and we drive off with some good-looking guys. I don't know where we are going, as it is pitch-black outside but I feel fine as I'm with Jackie. We arrive at a hip hop club to find that our names are already on the guest list. What a rush! I am rushing so much that my nipples are brick hard. I stand still and take in the dark smoky view which is a complete contrast to the bright florescent lights of the rave. I let the hip hop sound wash over me and I slowly start to move to the beat of the music. Dancing is the one thing that I can rely on in my life; it is always there for me and is the love of my life.

I feel another tap on my shoulder and Jackie tells me to follow her again. I follow her back to the car and we leave for yet another rave. What a night of extreme rushing, I am well high and loving every minute of it.

Me, Jackie and Busby decide to go to back to mine for a wee

smoke. I open the door really quietly and we all creep into my room. A musky smell hits me; it's one that I recognise but not from this house. I turn the light on and we can all hear strange sounds coming from my bed.

"What the fuck," I say as the light falls on my landlady who is fucking some rocker in my bed; nothing is mine in this world.

"I am fucking paying rent for that bed so I can sleep in it not so that you can fuck in it!" I say.

"Fuck you! My friend needed my bed, go and sleep on the sofa," shouts my landlady.

I take myself and my mates into the living room.

"What fucking shit! I need to find a real house to live in; fuck this shit."

We all go back to Busby's for the night where I proceed to drink a bottle of Buckfast and have about thirty spats on a bar fire then pass out for a wee while. The hooses here seem to be pure Farvo with coal and bar fires all of which smell of damp. Busby tells us about a guy called Ginger who beats his mum and dad and tells them to go to their bed so that he can then have a party in their house. The following day I go to View to see if there has been any word on this flat that this guy said I can stay in.

I manage to sort the flat out that is behind Marley's place. I share it with this guy, but he is never there as he stays with his mother in View. I am sorted. The flat is nice and clean and the only thing missing is food in the cupboards. All I have in my wee kitchen is some jam and bread, which I am bored of eating. I lean over the kitchen sink to look out of the window and I can see Marley hanging out her washing in the garden below me. The phone rings; it's a bolt out the blue, a call from my mother. I vaguely remember calling when I was high on jell eggs to let her know how fucked up my life had become; she must have saved my number! She starts telling me how George wants to take me on a fishing trip, he wants to build bridges or some kinda shit like that; I'm just thinking of the picnic as I'm always fucking hungry and I say yes please.

George picks me up the following day and we arrive at the riverside; I take a deep breath and feel the healing power of nature. It is beautiful here; the trees dip into the river causing the water to ripple and there is a faint breeze which passes over the river and me. Nature, the open space and the picnic help to take away the stress of what am I going to eat today.

I am enjoying the picnic; the sweet smell of flowers and fresh air are a far cry from the horrible Farvo smells. George is being kind to me but I always feel like he could go into flip mode any time. I have a go at fishing and manage to actually catch a fish; I thought it was a duck swimming across the line but no, wow it's a fish! I was the only one today to catch anything, and thank fuck. The heavens must have known I was starving. But George's childishness emerges after all as he hasn't caught a single fish all day. However his behaviour has no hold over me anymore whatsoever and I ignore him all the way home; it will take more than one fishing trip to fix our problem. I do miss my mum though.

"Thanks for the day out and thanks for the picnic; I was very hungry and now I have my tea," I say to George. It's such a delight when you catch your own food especially when you can't afford to buy any for yourself. I have grilled fresh trout and bread for dinner served with a large helping of satisfaction;

I sleep well with food in my belly. I steal a shot in my landlord's double bed tonight, as he is staying at his mum's. I enjoy having the whole of the bed to myself; I look at myself in the double mirrors at the end of the bed which adds to my satisfaction. It's always good to sleep well.

I am not quite sure what is happening to my stomach but I have terrible stomach pains every day. I have no time or understanding to listen to it; I only know that the lifestyle I am leading isn't a stable place to be in. I have no future thoughts on how I will ever be able to leave this life. Is there any other life for me? Anyway I haven't got the energy to cope with these feelings so I just internalise them and look forward to another party which is happening on Saturday night. I have no money and no drugs. Fuck! I have to take affirmative action. I've heard that if you go to the bottom of the high street at six in the morning you can get the Berry bus and earn some money by picking berries. So Ginger and I decide to give it a try. I wake up early and with my jam sandwiches and a half bottle of Buckfast I make my way to the bus with Ginger to go berry picking.

Today it is strawberry picking. On board the bus are a mixture of desperate druggies and families trying to supplement their income support. It's a sunny day and I always enjoy a visit to the countryside. As we are unloaded off the bus I can see rows upon rows of strawberries in the field and next to this field are rows upon rows of raspberries. I work hard for two hours; the spiky bushes tear my hands and the heat of unsheltered work takes its toll on my already tired puny body. When I finish my work I proudly take my punnet of strawberries to the till, admiring the sweet smell of fresh strawberries and they hand over £1.50

to me.

"What? £1.50 for two hours' work, that's worse than YTS wages," I say. I proceed to take out my blanket; jam sandwich and bottle of Buckfast. Fuck it, I think Ginger and I will just enjoy the sun and get a lie-in at the weekend.

"What the fuck do you think you are doing, young lassie?" asks the berry man. He is an old crumpled man with white hair and skin that has been wrinkled by the sun. I'm sure by his bad attitude he thinks that we are all desperate no hopers.
"What you think I'm doing? I'm having a picnic," I retort back.
"Denny think that you can come here and sit around, lassie; pick them fucking berries," he shouts at me as he is waves his crooked walking stick towards me.
"Your wages are worse than YTS wages, so you can fuck off old man and give me peace, I don't work for such shit wages."
"You and Ginger will no be getting on my berry bus again, lassie."
"Look old fucker, do you really think that Ginger and I will be getting on your berry bus again? You must be joking!"
I just chill all afternoon until the bus comes to take us home. When I get back to Farvo I decide to go and visit Marley with Ginger. I knock on her door and Jackie answers it dressed in a Pakistani suit.
"What's with the new clothes?" I ask her, puzzled by her appearance.
"Come in and we will show you!"
As we enter Marley's living room I see many of my friends who are dressed strangely.
"What's going on?" I ask.

132

"There's this salesman who keeps coming and hassling Marley. He always wants her to buy something so we thought we would give him a shock," explains Jackie.

"Come in and join us," says Marley. "Here, have a hairbrush and sing into it when he comes in."

I come in and sit down. I wonder to myself if it's the early morning or the sun which has affected my brain. The door bell goes and a guy called Michel who is dressed in jeans and a white T-shirt answers it.

"Hello, is Marley in today?" enquires the salesman.

"Yeah please come in, we have all heard aboot your wares and are very interested."

The salesman walks into the living room; he sees that Jackie is sitting on a rug in the middle of the room in a Pakistani suit. She has a missing tooth and is humming and chanting. Marley and I are sitting on the sofa across the room just under the window singing Mich Holt into our hairbrushes. Busby and Alli are also singing along with us and are jigging up and down on two chairs which are behind the door; they are both wearing mad hippy suits. On the bar opposite to us is a big black vibrator called Bully Boy which is set to vibrate and it is bouncing up and down. The salesman is just about to turn on his heels and run but Mich blocks his way so he can't escape.

"What is it you wanted to show me?" Marley asks him.

"Oh um I have another appointment I have to be at; I am sorry," says the salesman as he desperately pushes past Mich and quickly disappears. He looks really freaked out by what he has just seen, he never did come back to finish his sales pitch.

I think that I might have held too many parties in my nice two-bedroom flat, as my landlord throws me out; fuck I'm homeless again!

Busby tells me that I can stay with him and Ginger. They live in a flat in Farvo Circle close to where Robbie Tucker the local newsagent and Buckfast supplier is. I sleep on the sofa with a knife under my pillow as they are both dodgy; it's better than a freezing stairwell though. They like to have a laugh at my expense and sometimes when I come home they pretend that they aren't in. They like to watch me climb two flights up a drainpipe while I am often out of my head on drink and drugs. I always end up falling in through the bathroom window and on to the toilet just so I can have the sofa to sleep on. One particular night I am woken up by Busby saying to me, "Look out the window."

"What's going on like?" I ask.

"Look over there; Robbie Tuckers is being robbed."

We watch for about three hours as these two well known junkies rob his shop. We see them coming back and forth for more and then we see them leave with the safe. There isn't any movement over at his shop for over an hour so we decide to move in. It's about five in the morning now and as we walk up to the back of the shop we can see that the shutters have been ripped out and some of the brick wall has been knocked down. We step over all the rubble and we pass the back door which is lying on the floor. I look up and see where the safe used to be but there is rubble everywhere. What a weird sensation walking about in the shop when all the lights are out; it's a place that we come to almost every day, it is always tidy and bustling with loads of people.

But now there is an eerie silence and there is mess everywhere that we look. We have the pickings of what we want.

"Let's get to work," Busby says to us.

I have a green duffell jacket on that is perfect for when I go robbing. It has a tie cord around the waist and big sleeves with tight wrists which I fill with bacon, bread, apples and the week's groceries, I am hungry!

Ginger and Busby start to nick big bottles of whisky and vodka and I help myself to some ciggies. We keep going back and forth from Busby and Ginger's flat to the shop till about 6:30 a.m., then we have to stash our gear. We first stash it in the coal shed under an old rotten carpet which is next door to the flat; a couple of hours later we find a friend's car and stash it in the boot of his car. After all the excitement we go home, we play cards, we get pissed on a load of whisky and smoke some dope. Ginger makes a poor attempt to chat me up; he moves close up to my mouth and tries to kiss me. I have this uncontrollable retching feeling and I run quickly to try and get to the toilet, but I only get as far as the stairs and I start to throw up (my sick contains pure alcohol). Ginger is slightly offended by my reaction but he soon forgets all about it and goes off to bed drunk. The next thing I know I am woken up by a loud bang on the door.

"This is a bust, we are coming in now," shouts a loud voice.

I have no time to react, especially as I am hungover. The next thing I see is a tall policeman looming over me; he has moved the coffee table away from the sofa so that it is facing towards me.

"What you want?" I ask the police officers who have started to search the flat by this point.

"This is a product of a robbery," and he picks up the packet of ciggies from the coffee table just in front of me. You see Busby and Ginger are regular visitors to the local police station so it seems that this is their first stop to investigate the robbery.

Ginger comes into the room and they begin to check his coat pockets which have the coal shed keys in.

"What's this key to?" asks the policeman.

"I denny ken, it's no mine!" says Ginger.

"If it's no yours then why is it in your pocket?"

Busby and I turn and look at each other then back at the policeman. The bastard, he's trying to cheat us.

"Let's check, I bet it's the key to the coal cupboard," says the policeman. The sweat starts to coagulate around my chest; my heart is pounding, my mouth is getting dry and I feel like I am going to be sick. I'm pretty sure we cleared out the coal shed but Ginger was the last one in there and he had the key; why did he have the key? A carousel of thoughts run through my head as the policeman gives the key to his colleague and they go off to check the coal shed. Of course they find a big bottle of vodka and whisky; Ginger had been trying to con Busby and me and keep some of the stuff for himself.

"We hereby arrest you on suspicion of robbery." The policeman starts cuffing me and moves me towards the alcove between the living room and the unused dining room.

Ginger makes a run for it; he jumps on the sofa and straight out of the window, he is gone. As the policeman manhandles me though the alcove we go past the fruit bowl which is full of the stolen fresh fruit. I smile to myself and watch them as they start to rummage through the fridge and go right past the stolen bacon, eggs and butter. Busby and I are bundled into the police van which takes us to Cowden cells. The cells smell of piss; I am surprised to see toilets in these cells as Dunfy have no toilets in them, well, none that I can remember but I am always out of it when I visit them. I laugh as I remember my surprise and delight when a policeman passed by all the fresh food and fruit that I had stolen when they were arresting me. What makes the police think that a couple of jakies can afford to have all that food in their flat? Great! At least I won't starve tonight when I get out of here.

I am now sat in a questioning room which is a minging yellow colour with a desk reminiscent of my school days.

"Please sit down, Miss Brown." The policewoman signals to a brown square chair at the opposite side of the desk to her. As I sit down I notice a faint smell of disinfectant.

"Miss Brown, do you know how serious this whole situation is?"

"What do you mean?" I say, "I had nothing to do with anything."

"But we have found these cigarettes in your flat."

"That means nothing to me. I bought them yesterday."

"What happened last night, Miss Brown? Do you know you are up for a £5,000 robbery?"

A picture enters into my head. I am remembering seeing the shutters of the shop and there is no way a six-stone emaciated girl could perform such a robbery.

"Look, I was just sleeping when your colleague woke me up and busted me for what I denny ken."

"Are you aware, Miss Brown, that Robbie Tuckers' newsagents was robbed early this morning and the police found bottles of alcohol that were stolen from there last night in your shed?"

"That isny my shed so I am sorry I cannie help ya! I already told you I was asleep."

"We can fingerprint the bottles and if we find your prints on them you could do some serious time, Miss Brown, I mean two to three years."

I quickly run through my head how much contact I had had with the bottles; this is really hard to do as my head is very foggy with a hangover and tiredness. But I clearly remember that I only touched the ones that we put in the car.

"I have notin' to say, can you let me go now please?"

They put me back in the cells and offer me some dry ham rolls, which I take and use to block the toilets up with. Five hours later I have been released only to find that Busby had been let out a lot earlier than me. I wonder how he managed to get out so quickly. He is nowhere to be seen, so I catch a bus back to Farvo. I run into him as soon as I step off the bus and he hands over £20 to me for all the goods.

"What, £20? There was a lot more stuff than that, where's the rest of the money?" I ask him.

"Na! That's all I got for it – £60, £20 each. I couldn'y get much cash for it cos it's hot stuff man."

The bastard has robbed me; I can't trust anyone in this world. I think nothing of him getting let out early but the one thing I will not be accused of is being a grass. Something strange starts to happen. Every corner that I turn I see the two junkies that robbed the shop; they are following me with knives which flash in the sunlight and they look like the walking dead who are ready to kill with nothing to lose. I walk down one street and they are there saying they are going to stick me, then I turn another street and they are there again. I knew I hadn't grassed on them; I didn't even know them, that's when it hit me Busby was the grass. I'm getting threats left, right and centre that I am going to get my throat slit for being a grass, so I decide that the only way to solve this shit is to square up to Busby. I arrange a showdown with Busby in the Circle. It's dusk and the street lights are coming on; there are some scary faces in the crowd that have joined us. The street lighting highlights all the emaciated people gnarly in the dusk who are all thirsty for some savage action. Busby arrives kicking an old empty can of coke across at me then flicking his fag end across my head.

"I'll kick your fucking balls you grassing bastard and show you that I'm innocent," I yell at him.

"Fuck you, you are the grass," says Busby.

The crowd is growing and becoming more restless now and I will fight because it looks like I will die by his knife if I don't.

"Come on motherfucker, you know I didn't grass. I told the police that I was too emaciated to carry out such a crime and that I know nothing. You and Ginger bumped me, I got £20 from the whole thing."

The crowd start to chant "Fight, fight."

As I am about to fight the motherfucker he steps back and sticks a six-foot nutter in between us; this bloke has a reputation as a complete acid casualty.

"If you want me you have to go through him," says Busby.

"See, you are a motherfucking coward, that's why you need a big guy to fight your battles against a six-stone girl," I shout at him.

"You are the fucking grass, not me."

The crowd joins in, "Busby come on, she's a wee lassie, you'll kick her ass easy." They then shout, "You are a wee grassing prick, you coward, look at you." The junkies must all believe me because the only person being chased now is Busby. I am respected once again in Farvo; I am safe to go around the streets.

The next morning is nice and sunny and I am homeless again. I decide to get a crew together and we head up to Farvo woods with a whole pile of magic mushrooms, a stereo and a half bottle of whisky. We are all dancing as we make our way up the stony dusty path. To either side of us there are lots of trees and the sun beats down on the path which winds up to a field with a horse in it. We pass the horse, bidding our farewells after a wee petting; then we make our way deeper and further into the woods. We come across a rusty iron gate that is attached to a stone wall which towers above us all. Unable to resist the temptation, I open the gate and as I do so it makes an eerie creaking sound.

We slowly enter the garden which is just like some magical enchanted garden. There are streams and little rocks to bounce over which are all surrounded by the big stone wall and an old house is tucked away far across the other side of the garden. The garden reminds me of the land in the story of Narnia. After being granted the capacity to live again I believe that being able to enjoy this garden must be my reward. We all climb up a crab apple tree to get on to the wall; the tree nearly breaks free from the ropes that attach it to the wall under all of our weight. We dance on the walls; we climb and chew on crab apples which are so bitter that we immediately start spitting them out, but it is fun. We put the stereo on and dance to the hip hop sounds. What a lovely sunny day it is and as I look up I can see the valley spread out before me like a green and brown patchwork quilt. I can even see Logell Country Park and its waters. My thoughts are broken when Jackie asks me, "Have you found Farvo beach yet?"

"What?" Farvo beach is a longstanding mystery of Farvo and one that I will never have the chance to solve, as I know that after this close miss with death I need to leave Farvo. I don't know who is my friend or my enemy as they all smile at me. There are some guys up town who may have a lead on a place, so I let this thought pass and return to enjoy the sunshine and the beautiful view. Tomorrow is another day and who knows where I will sleep tonight; maybe I will just bed down here for the night.

The next day I go to investigate the lead on the flat. I really wish that I could have a shower, I feel so clogged up and sweaty. I don't like my smell. I will have to try and find a toilet in town so that I can freshen up. I have no self-confidence like this and I need it to get this flat. I catch up with some mates in town over some drinks and I manage to get a deal on a one-bedroom flat in Weir. A guy called Graham owns it. I don't even know what the place looks like or where it is, all I know is that it is in the countryside and that the guy will want housing benefit from me. This is what I need, as it sure beats wandering around exhausted and smelly.

CHAPTER 7

Strung out on the Line

Need to get out of this party scene. I am taking too much and puking blood. I don't know who are my friends and who are my enemies. Graham said he had a flat in Weir, away out in the countryside, there only five houses in a row.

I will rent it off him for a while; I don't know what will happen to me but I am ready to explode all over Farvo. If I denny go I feel my life resonating at such a high level, I feel if I don't act soon I am going to die. So I agree to rent it and off I go, moving into the one-bedroom flat alone. I got a lot of nice drapes given to me by Jacob, a friend. I had to sort out the rent and council stuff and God knows how I have managed this. I am in a daze, I am just living but I feel like I don't really exist. It is like my soul is completely dying and there is barely a flicker of light left in me.

Should a strong wind blow I will be gone!

Luckily I am used to dealing with the dole as I have been in the system for a

while now.

I arrive at my flat all alone with severe drug and mental problems. I am so sad

and damaged; I do not know why I am here but I feel that no one cares anyway so why should I? I am just waiting for death. May as well be here than anywhere else. I don't know what to eat. My diet usually consists of bread and drugs; I get some packet cheesy pasta and loads of tins. I begin to feel a pinch in my mind, a need, I want something. I need something, what is it? I am struggling with a hunger, a need that is not going to be met; I am sweating now, it is dripping off me. I am dizzy and there is a carousel of words going around in my head. My stomach is producing violent convulsions and I feel I am falling apart; I need to get to the toilet fast. I try to see it through my sweat and tears, I am bent over holding on to anything I can that will help me get there.

Ahh!! The pain is ripping through my brain, the saliva is building up in my mouth, my jaw is struggling to stay shut then my mouth violently opens wide, my knees retracted to my stomach like they were on springs. I am now kneeling on the toilet and my insides are being deposited in the toilet along with the blood. Oh shit! I must swing around as it is coming from the other end now. Help me, I am so scared, help me! There is no one here to hear my cries; I am alone and scared. Finally the feelings subside and I crawl to my sofa and curl up in a ball. I am again waiting for death, surely it can't be long. I roll a joint and try to chill by putting on loud music to drown out me. I am unwashed and in pain and I find myself waking up on the sofa where I must have passed out. I don't know how long this has been going on. Days? Weeks? I don't know. I have used my stereo so much the amp is not working and I am frantically unscrewing it to try and fix it. The time it takes occupies my mind and I manage to do it. Ah! Thank fuck, music again; I would lynch myself if I don't have music to get me through this madness. I smoke heavy on the dope, it seems to ease my pain but I am running out so I must stick myself together, make myself look like I am OK and go score some dope otherwise lynching becomes the only way.

I go visit some friends in Kidimister. They are all getting ready to go to a rave called Resurrection.
"Why don't you join us, Katie?" asks Halle.
"I was just after a wee smoke and am going back to chill," I reply.

"But why, where you living at the moment?"

"I've got a wee house in Weir," I respond.

"What, you living on your own like?"

"Yes."

"Well denny be silly, come out wi' us and go and chill tomorrow!"

"I denny have any money," I say.

"Fuck it, we've got plenty drugs and we'll get you in."

"OK I will come, it canny do any harm," I say. No sooner had the words been spoken than I was in a convoy of cars off to the Rez, me and twelve guys.

When we arrive we drop an E each and wait in the extended queue. It is fucking freezing and I am a wee waif, I denny ken how I am standing. I have been here before and my mind is going back to those times. My thoughts are broken; as we come to the door we are searched and let in. I am having a ball because for these few hours my troubles and craziness of the weeks before cease to exist as the peace that comes with Ecstasy takes it away. This is why I like it. I forget all the hardness and coldness of life and everyone loves everyone else.

"Katie de ya want some speed?"

"Aye OK," I say and out comes my adapted nail, one which I have grown so long to scoop up the drugs. I scoop a nail-full and then I snort it up my nose. There is a shudder that moves from my nose down the back of my throat, the feeling goes down my spine and kinda explodes into my system. I feel a twinge in my stomach but I refuse to listen, I am coming up so high I feel that I may hover around the Rez. I disappear into the dance floor and as I do I look around me and see people sucking dummies with wide saucer eyes, light sticks waving everywhere and dance moves that seem to defy any kinda logic of movement or gravity. Oh no, jittery jaw, my mouth is moving up and down ninety to the dozen. I need to be careful not to bite my tongue off. I am coming up more and more. I dance the night away and it feels great.

I find myself dealing with the toilet again, vomiting blood with puke twice already and I know this is not good. In the car on the way home my stomach is cutting with pain. I know I am coming down and I know this night was a mistake but I look on the positive side of it, at least I enjoyed the dance. I am silent for the duration of the journey.

"You coming back to ours, Katie?"
"Yeh that would be good, get a smoke eh?"
"Cool."
We arrive back in Kidimister and I am back on a buzz and, being wide, I love the mentalities of some men. We take the lift and are packed in like sardines all the way to the 13th floor of the high rise.
"Be quiet when you pass Jimmy's room, he will be asleep."
"Come on, let's get the bong out and get stoned!" I say.
"Let's skin up!"
Twelve of us smoke bongs, pipes, joints; we smoke till the point that one by one the boys start to fall asleep. There are three of us awake and no dope, just the housemate's hash plant looking very afraid at the end of the living room. We look at it, then at each other.
"No don't, it's my flatmate's, he will kill me."
"Ah come on, we will just have a few leaves, he won't notice."
"Just a couple then, no more!"

Before we know it there is a bare stalk and just me awake with a joint in my hand. They call me the bucket queen because I can smoke like a motherfucker. Jimmy opens the door and sees me sitting in a room full of sleeping men and with a joint in my hand. He turns to his plant. The colour drains from his face, I see a rise of a red colour in his face and suddenly a loud cry issues from his mouth.

"You fucking smoked my fucking plant, get out all of you bastards, fucking out!" Jimmy screams at us while making a concerted effort to kick the sleeping occupants of his house. I assess it's time to leave. I go past the town and get hold of some dope to take back to Weir. As I fall asleep on the bus I realise that I have a defence mechanism that would not let me sleep in a room full of men.

I am all set up for another bad comedown. I have food, music and dope so I have a shower and change then I get stoned and go to bed. The feeling of my soft covers is bliss; it doesn't take long for sleep to arrive.

The next day is rent day and I know Graham will be round so I go to the cash machine and get his cash and some bacon, eggs and rolls then go back to the flat. Graham arrives about tea-time.

"Hello, how are you Katie?" says Graham.

"Ah! You know am doing away!" I say.

"How's the flat for you?" he asks.

"Oh it is a godsend thanks, I am enjoying it," I reply.

"It's a bit of a trek into town though eh?" asks Graham.

"Yeh! Here is your rent Graham," I say, handing him his money.

"Thanks! You busy at the weekend?" he asks.

"Notin' planned," I respond.

"Duncan is having a birthday party, why don't you come? I am going to Edinburgh in the week, I have got a good deal on some shit-hot microdots. £1 each if you buy in bulk, that's cheap for acid, eh? Do you want some, I'm sure you could shift them easy and make a wee profit?" asks Graham.

"Aye OK I will take 30, shall I just bring the money on Friday to the party?" I ask. (As I hear the words fall out my mouth I listen in disbelief; 'you are meant to be stopping, Katie' I think to myself.)

"I will need the money up front, you can trust me, you are in my house, you know what I'm saying!" says Graham.

"I can only give you the money on Sat, I will need to get some orders this week, that's all I can do, I have no money," I tell him.

"I know what, I will take it off this month's rent and you will owe me £30 rent, OK?" says Graham.

"OK let's do that."

The week goes pretty fast and I get my customers and head off to the party on the Friday night. As I arrive at Duncan and Matthew's house all I can hear is arguing and fighting. This is no surprise to me as this couple always argued. There are more people at the party; there is Duggy and Mich and some other people that I don't know. The party is getting started and Duncan and Matthew kissed and made up. The fire is on in the living room and I am relatively chilled. The door goes so I say I will get it and to my horror Daniel is on the other side of it with some blonde woman on his arm. I swallow my hate and hurt and welcome them in. I hate her already as she is with Daniel. She doesn't look like she is enjoying herself, anyway she doesn't really speak and looks like a shell of a person. Daniel tries to make small talk but inside I am raging. Much to my relief Graham arrives with his girlfriend from Edinburgh. He seems so loved up with her. I see another guy kinda fall in behind them who looks in a bad way. He mumbles something about the toilet and disappears.

"Here, come into the kitchen Katie, I've got somethin' for you," gestures Graham.

Relieved for a reason to leave Daniel and his bitch, I follow Graham past the banister into the blue kitchen.

"I could only get you 15 and they are £2 each," he says to me.

"I need the £15 Graham, I agreed £1 each you, canny change now," I begin to protest.

"It was hard for me to get them," says Graham.

"You told me the guy had loads, this is dodgy!" I say.

"Eh Katie! Don't fucking get me started," says Graham, his voice with a threatening sound to it.

"I've been all over fucking Edinburgh to get these for you and I let you stay in my house, do you think I would be fucking you? I could always find someone else to rent my flat you know! Do you want them or not?"

"Yes that's fine, sorry about that," I say for fear of being homeless again and having no proof anyway.

"That's all right, I understand, sorry I couldn't get them cheaper for you," Graham apologises.

Personally I think he is a scheming lying bastard but I am backed into yet another corner. I drop one of the microdots; I soon realise this is a bad mistake as my mind starts to warp. I don't seem to enjoy this anymore but why do I still take it? The answer is beyond me.

I look around me as I enter the living room and I think everyone is laughing at me as I have just been ripped off. I can see Daniel with his big smile that says 'don't tell anyone what I put you through'. I can no longer stand it and I leave, heading for the time bomb that I call home.

I am nearly home now, feel safer, it is a nice walk from the bus stop to my house past a field and a graveyard. I enjoy my acid as I watch the space around me and the movements of the clouds. I notice a black cat in the shadows and I befriend her and she follows me home. I get home and give her some milk and decide to call her Ecy so that I would always have an E in the house when I need one. I chill all Saturday morning on a comedown but it's better than that crazy party; all my paranoia is starting to settle. I have a bucket then another and am starting to feel a wee bitty more level. I must eat at some point, it has been a day at least since I last ate but I am not hungry so I will have another bucket. Am starting to feel sick again, oh no, not again, why do I keep putting myself through this? I find myself crouching on the toilet seat again and the blood, sweat and tears are back. I am numb, I don't seem to care about anything, even the pain, anymore; I certainly don't care about myself. I eat some toast to soak up the acid in my stomach. I feel like I am going to be sick again. I don't think I could take another boat so I put music on and try to distract my mind. I put some toothpaste in my mouth to disguise the flavour of my stomach.

The door goes and it makes me jump; I wonder who it could be as not many people know I live here. I casually go to the door and look out the window; it is Daniel!
"Hello," he says.
"Hi," I manage to say, still in shock that it is him at the door. I thought he had finished with me.

"Can I come in? I didn't come here to stand on the doorstep, Katie, I came to see you," says Daniel. I move aside and let him past. As he walks past me I can smell his cologne and I remember how much I fancy him. It's as if I have memory loss because all I feel is so lucky that he has come to visit me; 'he must like me' I start to think.

"I am sorry about last night! She was just a friend so I couldn't really talk. I was worried when you disappeared but I had already promised to take her home to Edinburgh so I couldn't come after you," explains Daniel.

I don't say anything to disturb him in case he leaves as I am enjoying having him here. I am slightly besotted by him and all his words just soak into my brain and I believe everything he says.

"I missed you last night, Katie," says Daniel. "Here, I brought you a wee present, you want to skin up?"

"Yes that would be nice, thank you," I respond as I take the lump of dope that is being offered me then proceed to skin up.

I can see Daniel pulling a bag out of his pocket.

"Do you want a line of coke?" he asks.

"I think I will leave it tonight, Daniel," I say, a flashback of me retching blood down the toilet coming back to my mind.

"Oh go on, just one wee line will do no harm, I will feel lonely having it on my own!" He is persuasive.

"OK." I hear my voice submitting to his request. It will be the last time definitely.

"There, this will be good," says Daniel as he hands me the mirror with two lines on it and a rolled-up note. I put it close to my face and I can see my reflection in the mirror as I snort this drug. I can see my face is tired, I don't know what he sees in me.

"You look so sexy, Katie," he says to me.

"You're mad, I've been on a comedown all day and was upset at the party."

"I thought you were upset at the party, that's why I came here today," he explains as he pulls me close and gives me a warm cuddle. I can smell the warmth of his body and the smell of his cologne; I can feel the beat of his heart racing with the coke. I could stay in this cuddle forever.

"Here, have another line," he says.

"I am OK, I said I am just enjoying the cuddle."

"Come on girl, the cuddle will feel twice as good with another line too," urges Daniel.

I see my face again in the mirror, I am lying to myself, I am convincing myself that what he says is true. What is going on? I am desperate for love. The thoughts soon leave as the coke hits my brain and I feel warm all over and Daniel is nuzzling at my neck. I am becoming more confused with the truth, coke and the signals Daniel is giving. My stomach and mind are protesting but I am falling into his body again. I know he is no good for me but I have no strength to say no.

He is kissing me and I respond with vigour, it seems as if it's the only loving I will be getting. He moves my hand over his trousers and his cock is hard; I am becoming more turned on by the minute. He is easing my clothes off me, then he strips back and reveals his body and his big hard cock. He leans down and I feel myself opening, ready to receive him inside me. As he moves in and out of me I think I could ride this baby all night.

I am a horny, lonely lady and he is my chance to serve these needs, I tell myself to try and make myself feel better as the sickening thought keeps coming in that he was with his blonde friend last night.

He comes inside me and withdraws; I lie there cold and naked, exposed on the bed.

"I have to go, sorry, as I have business to take care of, you know how it is!" He is getting dressed and ready to leave. This hits me right in the heart and mind.

"Oh!" I respond weakly.

"Will call again soon, OK, bye," he says and is gone.

"OK bye."

I am in shock, I feel so used. His dick is barely cold and he has gone and I am lying in a crazy dazed state on my bed. The coke is wearing off and the night is rolling in. I curl up into the foetal position. Shit! Silly bitch! You were supposed to say no! No! Stupid bitch! Slag! Stupid slag! All the words from my stepfather come back to me; I am convinced he was right, I really am worthless and nobody will be my friend unless I give them something. My equilibrium has left me. The pain in my stomach is bad now, more of a comedown. How will I ever free myself of the thought of when I was 15 and raped and the mentality of just giving in and letting people abuse me? How will I ever be free? I feel used, he just comes in and says some things and flaunts his cock then fucks me and leaves; this life is shit! I need to learn how to say NO! NO! NO! NO! NO! I am shouting at myself in the mirror looking at this thin damaged girl. HELP ME! I'm fucked.

I am violently sick again. The pain I feel is punishment for being such a gullible bitch. It subsides and I have a bucket. I pass out, God knows when. Next thing I know my eyes are open and it is Sunday; I feel pain in my stomach, my heart and my pussy. He is a big man and it is hard to pee. I must eat, but toast is all I can be bothered to make, it seems this is all I eat. I try to sleep the day away. I don't want to be here and I hope I can sleep it all away until a better day or death.

I hear a knock at the door and it makes me jump. The thought crosses my mind that maybe it is Daniel back. I get up and walk through the living room to go to the back door. When I open it there is nobody there, maybe it is my mind playing tricks on me? Then I hear another knock at the front door so I walk back through the living room through the bedroom to the hall and open the door. The colour drains from my face and I feel myself starting to sweat, my heart is beating till I feel I am going to pass out.

There in front of me looking very serious are two policemen and one policewoman.

"Is this Graham Rider's place?" asks the male police officer.

"Yes," I manage to stammer out.

"Can we come in please?" he asks.

"Why? You can't just walk in, he doesn't live here, I live alone," I reply.

"We have a warrant to search the premises," says the officer as he moves me aside and walks in followed by his colleagues. I remember the 14 microdots on my fireplace and I start to feel even sicker. The police start searching my possessions.

"Graham doesn't live here, I am renting it. Surely there is a law against this intrusion?" I say, hoping they will stop and leave. The female police officer sits next to me.

"Is there anything you want, like, to tell us before we find it?"

she asks.

"No!"

The sweat is building up as I see them getting closer, I am panicking now.

"Are you all right, Miss Brown, you look awfully pale?" she asks.

Fear and madness take over me and I jump up and lunge for the pillbox containing the microdots and I try to swallow them, hoping to get away. I get as far as the door to my bedroom and I can see out the corner of my eye the policeman lunging at me and I hear the female officer shout, "She's got something she is trying to swallow." I desperately try to swallow the pillbox but it is too big; I plan to open it and swallow the microdots when I feel a strong hand around my jugular and my breathing is constricted. A hand is on my nose and then one officer on each arm. I can't move and I can't breathe; their combined strength and my weakness take over, I am their prisoner.

The male officer shouts, "Spit it out you stupid girl, spit it out." I open my mouth in the fight for some air and the pillbox falls out into the female's open hand. It is still shut.

"You got anything else?" asks the policeman.

"No," I say as I am held in a star position by the other officers.

"Are you going to be sensible now? Strip-search her!" says the male officer to the female officer, then he turns away into the living room to continue his search.

"Could you please come in the room and take off your clothes?" she asks me as she shuts my bedroom door behind me.

"Do I have to? I have nothing else," I protest.

"Yes I am afraid so, right down to your birthday suit please," she states.

"We've found something!" shouts one of the other officers.

My heart jumps and all sorts of thoughts rush through my head. Did Graham or Daniel leave anything? Is this a set-up? Am I going to end up in jail? I feel like I am going to go mad.

"Bag them," I hear the officer say.

I am allowed to put my clothes back on and am guided into the living room, now I am made to sit down on the sofa. "Are these your scales?" asks the officer.

"Yes," I reply.

"And this £20?"

"Yes."

"Well Miss Brown, you will need to lock up the house as you will be coming with us tonight," the officer states.

I lock up and am immediately under their control as I am forced into the police car to sit next to her.

"Do you want to die?" asks one of the officers.

"No," I say and I am worried. I think maybe this is a set-up and they are going to kill me.

"If you had managed to swallow that pillbox you would either die or be in a mental institution – is that what you want, you silly girl?"

"Thank you for your concern," I say sarcastically.

I am shitting myself with fear, I am so scared to go to jail. I am praying to someone, anyone, to save me. I am taken out the car to the checking desk where I have been before. My prints are taken and my personal effects bagged, after which I am shown to the magnolia cells.

"Take care and think about what you are doing before it is too late," the officer says and then he is gone.

Back to the mattress as thin as a matchstick and a coarse blanket; I am left here with the power of my fear and own thoughts. The night lasts for what seems like forever. I wonder how long I will be in here, last time it was three days without charge. I am scared. I jump as the shutter to the door opens and I see a male officer standing there.

"Here is some soup for you," he says

"I don't want to eat."

"Court is not on 'til Tuesday, you better eat or you will disappear," and with that he leaves.

I spend Sunday and Monday night in this hell hole with only the sounds of doors banging and shouts of abuse from other inmates. I feel like a dog in a cage and the food is shit. I am so scared, I don't want to go to jail and be fucked with cucumbers by some freaky dyke!!

I jump. I don't know if I slept and what time it is but it is still dark; the sound of the surge of electricity powers the powerful strip light in my cell. I can't see anything but a tall man's shape in the light and my cell is open.

"Come girl, it is court time," he says. I am guided along a maze of hallways all strip lights and magnolia.

I have never been up in the court cells before; the room is quite big and full of women, maybe ten. The walls are brick, painted magnolia, they must have got an afy good deal at B&Q on that magnolia shit. I look at the blue lino floor and the benches along the walls and up the middle. I put on my 'I'm hard as fuck' exterior, it doesn't pay to show weakness here. I take a seat and I feel the fear in the air along with the tiredness, then I hear men.

It makes me jump before I realise there is a cell next door men.

"What you in for?"

I turn around and a woman is sitting next to me.

"Supply, concern of supply, intent to supply, possession and obstruction of justice. And you?" I ask.

"Theft. Don't worry, I am in and out of here every week."

"I have not been here before, what's the procedure?" I ask her.

"In theory they will keep you in here until your case is heard, if you're lucky it will be today, then they will let you go on a good behaviour bond," she explains.

This day is one of the longest I have known; one by one the women and men are being called up before the judges. It feels like black sheep to the slaughter. The men are becoming more rowdy as the day goes on and they are shouting comments like, "I like your pussy," "I will come there and fuck you up the arse!" I shout back, "Fuck you, you limpdick arseholes."

"That's enough," the cell guard tells me. I am becoming more and more agitated as the day passes; I have no idea of the time. As the men pass the cell on their way to court they tease the women. Before long I am the only one left. What is going on?

"Come on, you will have to wait till tomorrow, it is always busy after bank holiday weekend, you will get your turn tomorrow," explains the officer as I am led dazed along the magnolia maze back to my kennel where I am offered some salty soup.

"Fucking bastards, not another night of this shit," I protest.

My body is thin and bruised by the shit cover the mattress provides against the stark floor. I jump up, I don't know if I slept it it is dark. I hear the sound as the surge of e powerful strip light in my cell. I can't see in's shape in the light and my cell is open. t time again, maybe it's your lucky day, .ull today," he says, guiding me along a maze of ...ways, all strip lights and magnolia.

He is right, I am the only woman in the cellblock today so I am up at court by lunchtime. When I am taken to court I pass the men's cell and all I hear are taunts of, "I will rip your nipples off and fuck you, bitch."

"Fuck off boy, you would die trying," I shout.

"OK that's enough," the guard warns.

"Why you gonna let them talk to me like that then tell me to shut up?" I ask.

I stick my middle finger up at them. "Chew on this you jailed motherfucker," I say then I turn towards the court feeling hungry, tired and smelly after three nights of cold sweats in the cell/kennel.

I am presented to the judge and as I am standing in the dock and everything is big I feel so weak. All I hear are exchanges of mumbles then a hammer drops and the judge addresses me.

"Miss Brown, you have been found guilty of possession, concern of supply and obstruction of justice. I hereby sentence you to … (my heart nearly jumps out my mouth and the thought of cucumbers and mad dykes is whirling around in my head) … three hundred and twenty-one hours community service. You are free to go. The courts will be in touch in due course."

I hate how they never let me talk or defend myself. I am taken back to the cell block where my possessions are returned and I am then thrown out the police station in a state of shock.

When I get home I get in touch with some friends who tell me the only reason the police were at my door was because Graham had been caught drink-driving. His Edinburgh friend had jacked up a microdot and they were trying to get him to hospital, he was caught with dope and microdots on him. In the drug world when you cause someone to be busted you carry the charge. You don't leave it to them. He was already up on big charges and if he had carried over the 14 microdots found in my home – his house which was searched because of his stupidity – it would have made no difference to his time. But he is a yellow-bellied bastard and he just looked at me without a care and let me take the shit he had caused. I move out the next week and am homeless again. A friend called Dugy offers me a fold-out bed in his flat. The problem is it is in the living room of a flat with five punks and they are friends of Graham's, the shits just don't stop. One good thing though is it is not too far for my brother Bremner to come visit me. I love him so much, he really tries, he brings me a wee food parcel.

"How are you?" says Bremner.
"Feel like shit, if you must know!" I reply.
"Mum really wants to meet up with you, she is really upset about the court thing," he says with concern in his voice.
"I can't see her, I am broken and George is still with her so nothing will change, what's the point?"
"I just thought I would let you know. Nan is asking if she can write to this address, she wants to send you some pocket money," he continues.

"Aye that would be great!" I reply, happy that I may be able to get some more food. We exchange a big hug and my address, I feel tears in my eyes as he walks away. The tears change to pain in my stomach and heart; I try and pull myself together as I turn to walk up the stairs that lead to my new resting place. I am wondering 'how long will this one last?'

After some time staying here I decide to go to Glasgow for a party. I am so out of my head on drugs it takes me a week to get back. I don't seem to care that I am on a downward spiral to hell, no one seems to care. I find myself lying smoking loads of grass on my fold-out bed in Dugy's house, again just waiting to die.

I am consumed in my own misery and the sickness is back, not that anyone here seems to notice. I am lying here in a plume of grass smoke when I hear my name called.

"Katie! Katie!"

"Hello!" I reply.

"Hello, how you doing Katie, it's me Liam, we used to go to school together."

"Oh OK, how you doing?"

"I am good, I am living in Edinburgh now," says Liam, "this is my mate Jed."

"Hi, how you doing?" I ask.

"We have space in our flat in Edinburgh, if you fancy staying you are welcome," he says.

I am well aware my welcome is wearing out in this flat, I mean who wants a sick, fucked up girl sleeping in their living room? So I decide there is nothing else for it but to move on again. I don't think I will be walking too much longer anyway because I am sick and tired of life.

CHAPTER 8

Hotel Paradiso

It is moving day and I have arrived in Edinburgh in a hired van that Gerome has managed to get hold of.

These guys are so nice to me and they all say they know me but I cannot remember who they are. I recall a few parties in a big flat in Edinburgh where there was a sauna, but my memory is a bit foggy.

Gerome crosses the traffic lights at Toll Cross junction and heads towards Brinton. He then takes a sharp left up a one-way street which has a pillow factory on the right and a nursery on the left. I spot two phone boxes next to the opening of the nursery; I will remember where they are. The street has trees lining the pavement and along the left hand side are a number of flats; the brickwork of the flats look very grand and impressive as the sun shines down on them. As we pull up to the door of the flat I wonder what this next phase of my life will bring. Will I survive much longer?

We buzz the intercom and Liam answers.

"Hello."

"Hi Liam it's us, is Shaun there to help us please?"

A smiling Liam arrives at the door.

"I will hold the door, sweetie; I don't think I am the right man to be lifting things, just go straight up one flight of stairs and it's the first door on your right, hunny, it's open," and he gestures for me to go inside.

"Do you want my help to lift anything?" I say before I go up to the flat.

"We are fine, just go and roll a joint," says Gerome.

As I walk into the front door I am greeted by a large square hall with various doors coming off of it.

I look to my immediate right where Shaun's room is and next door is Liam's room. They also live with a bloke called Decland. Decland is a punk and is kind enough to let me kip in their kitchen. The flat has lovely Georgian features: high ceilings, beautiful sash windows which let in loads of daylight and sturdy white wooden doors. I make my way to my new place of residence: a sofa bed which is next to a very noisy fridge in the corner of the kitchen. At least the kitchen has a wonderful big window that looks out on to a shared garden.

"Here you are," says Liam, "this is your space, what do you think?"

"I think it is a welcome relief. I will have to add a touch of Katie to make it my home, is that all right?"

"That's fine, do you want some help?"

Gerome interrupts us at this point as he struggles through the door with box of possessions.

"Katie, you could have packed it in two boxes! How much stuff you got in here?"

"I thought if I packed it all in one box it would be no problem!"

"Shaun and I nearly broke our backs moving it up the stairs."

"Sorry about that, I will know next time!"

"Next time! Next time! Do you think I will do it again?" Gerome shouts at me.

"Ah! Come on Gerome, you know you love me! Come and have a cup of tea and a joint."

Liam sits down to make a joint and I put the kettle on before I start to unpack and spread some of my Katie style in the kitchen corner!

"Can I put a washing line up across the corner here, Liam?"

"Sure hunny that's fine, why don't you let me help you?"

I look up at Liam and notice that he is a tall, dark, handsome man with a nice tight butt.

After a couple of hours of pulling various Indian drapes from my box of tricks and attaching them to the wall with a few pins and nails the kitchen corner is transformed.

"There! It is my space now."

"Wow," say all the blokes in a chorus.

"I will name it 'le boudoir'!" says Liam in a really bad French accent.

I stand back to admire our work; I have quickly sewed a hem on one of the drapes so I am able to thread the washing line through it. There is a divide in between the drapes now which is my door so that you can slide it back to enter le boudoir.

A colourful array of silvers, reds, greens and yellows welcomes you and all the walls of my little corner have been totally transformed by the vibrant pieces of material. There sat in amongst the array of colour is the brown sofa bed which I will roll out when it is time to sleep.

I have now settled into my new home and we all celebrate with a few joints and take some time to chill out.

After being here for a few weeks I start to notice things in this place, things I have never known before. We all go out clubbing together and so many people come round to the flat to hang out. We all dress in wild clothes and party. The drug intake here is less than I am used to and there is a scene of love all around me. People work hard all week and party hard at the weekends. Drug-taking is a weekend event and not a daily one.

My body starts to withdraw from the drugs slightly, but when the weekend comes round I take copious amounts of Ecstasy, about three to five of them. They always make me sick, but I always blame it on the dinner that I have just eaten.

One particular day when most of the occupants of the house are getting up and ready for work I am lying in the kitchen corner unable to move a muscle. The phone is ringing; I feel so bad and there is so much noise from the other housemates.

"Shut up for God's sake, how can I sleep?" I shout out in a rabid manner.

"What do you mean 'shut up'? Some of us have to work. We don't all get to lie around all day doing nothing!" shouts Liam.

I decide to go to the doctor's and try and get help for my pain. The female doctor must know that I am taking drugs. I convince myself that no one knows about my drug habit and I make out that I don't understand why I am so messed up. She prescribes me with various pills: some for my stomach, some for sleeping, some to stop my diarrhoea and pain; I rattle when I walk.

Liam arrives home that evening and says that he needs to talk to me. He goes on to say, "Katie, it's not the food that you eat that is making you ill, it's the drugs that you take. You have to stop taking them now, look at you! You are as skinny as a rake and sick as fuck!"

I know he is right.

"I will try, I will. I need our friendship, it is so supportive for me," I say.

"I have never seen someone take so much Ecstasy and not die, Katie. Look at the size of you; for Christ's sake do you want to die?" he is pleading.

"I know what you're saying is right, I know."

I am trying to break free from the drugs as the pain is getting worse every day. I am lying in the corner in so much pain. I am scared that I will die. I am throwing up blood all the time and my mind is on the edge between reality and nothingness. I am scared!

I am so full of anger and I am so moody that I fly off the handle at the slightest thing. I have reduced my illegal drug intake a lot from what I used to take, so what exactly is the next step? I don't know.

Am I gonna be useless?

Will I ever amount to anything more than maybe a shop assistant?

I have no idea how to relate to the real world. I have been down in this sub-life for so long! If I carry on like this I will die.

I start to go out clubbing at the weekends again. I wear one of my handmade outfits. I have taught myself how to sew with a sewing machine that a friend let me borrow.

We are all looking and feeling really good; I have my hair braided. The excitement begins to flow as we leave the flat and head to the taxi rank; there is no way you would get Liam on a bus. We all chip in for the taxi and before we know it we have arrived at the Shiva. Edinburgh city looks so beautiful; the city lights sparkle and our breath is visible in the cold night air.

Shiva is a shit-hot techno club which is set in an underground cave. We grab some seats in the corner, this will be our base for tonight.

I have an E in my pocket, just in case I need it. I will try to see if I can enjoy the night without taking it.

 I feel a tap on my shoulder and I turn around.

"All right Katie, what you on tonight?"

"Nothing."

"Fuck off, you are kidding me! You're on notin? Not likely," says Jess.

"No, honestly, I have had nothing."

"Why, can ye not get any like?"

"Yeah, I have one on me but I'm neh takin' it."

"Why not? Are you fucking mad! What one you got?"

"A Dennis the Menace," I say.

"They're fucking great! Take it now, denny be so mad! Anyway see you later, I'm off for a dance."

"Bye!"

I can feel the E in my pocket and I nearly pull it out to swallow it but I feel a sharp pain in my stomach, a stark reminder of why I'm trying not to take it. I look around me at the sea of people with wide eyes; there are sweaty emaciated bodies everywhere. Just beyond the bar I can see the toilet where I remember being sick a few years back; I nearly passed out and nobody came to help me!

I am starting to see now that I denny belong here; the place where I had spent years comfortably numb on drugs, dancing and false loving was now a scary place – busy but a very lonely place. I feel scared as I know now that I will have to walk away from yet another big illusion, alone into my unknown future.

It's an hour before the end of the club and I reach into my pocket and feel the E still there. It has been my security blanket all night, I remove it from my pocket and I look at the small white pill in the palm of my hand. I look around at the flashing lights which highlight the contorting faces and the frantically dancing mass of bodies. I raise my hand up and throw the E up into the air; it moves through the air in slow motion. I open my mouth wide and catch it in between my tongue and lips.

I wash it down with some water and wait for twenty minutes. It doesn't take long for the atmosphere to change around me. The edges of the room start to soften; the people seem so much friendlier and the lights are beautiful as they work in perfect time with the music. I feel the urge to dance and make my way to the dance floor.

I look through the dry ice and see Jess.

"Did you pop it?"

"Yeah."

"Fucking great, eh! Give us a big hug, man!"

We have a hug. As our sweaty emaciated bodies embrace I feel a mixture of excitement and euphoria. It's as if the DJ has just put the music on to welcome me back into the clutches of the madness that surrounds me. I dance, fully absorbed by the E, the lights and the music.

The next day Liam asks me, "Did you take it then?"

"Yes, at the end of the night. I went most of the night without it," I add.

"So why did you take it then?"

"I didn't want to waste it."

"What about your life and your health? You radge! Do you want to waste that?"

"One step at a time, Liam, one step at a time, I will try and not take one with me next weekend."

"Well I would like to see that," he exclaims.

The week passes really slowly and the pain in my stomach is bad but the drugs from the doctors are helping.

It is Saturday night and we are all getting ready to go out.

"What you doing, Katie?" Shaun asks me.

"I am making a packed lunch!"

"What! Are you mad?" he says, holding back his disbelief.

"Na man, I will be rocking on a salmon sandwich and an apple tonight, cos I'm hardcore!"

"You are a Fife radge!"

"My stomach hurts all the time and if I don't put something in it when it does I will fade away, maybe even faint."

"Good luck," Liam says.

We all do the usual and get a taxi to the club. I am nervous as I don't have an E for a security blanket tonight; all I have is my packed lunch.

I am paranoid. It is easier to just hide a sick mind with drugs; you kinda don't care. I leave my sandwich with some friends who are running a herbal Ecstasy fruit juice bar. I go off to enjoy the music and do some dancing.

At the club I bump into Jess again.

"What you on tonight Katie?" she asks me.

"A salmon sandwich and an apple."

The look I receive says it all. It's as if all the atoms in the world have collided in her brain, and after a minute of vacant staring Jess just turns around and disappears into the smoky crowd.

My life is changing again. My delusions are fading but the immense pain is still within my body. I am exhausted but I must follow my intuition and keep moving forward.

At least now I have given up on the idea that I will die in this sad life; there is a chance I may live.

CHAPTER 9

Up the Hill and Down the Dale

Finally, with the help of a friend saying I was biding at his hoose I have managed to get together enough money for rent and deposit for a flat in Rank Street. I can't believe it, I have a job! I knew that college course I done for Nursery Nurse would help me eventually so it wasn't all for nothing. Who would have thought – Katie with a job and now a house! I'm starting to feel a wee bitty more human.

Ah shit! Very short-lived as am too ill to work. I go to the nursery to work every day and I give it my all but the pain is too distracting and I am always going to the toilet to be sick. I am still losing blood in my vomit and when I am looking after the children it is hard when the pain rises; I am nearly incoherent, my ears become muffled and I become lightheaded. I have to let go of this job, I am just not well enough, when is my life going to ease up on me and let me chill?

The job's well and truly gone now and I am now in bed in my new flat; I just seem to be sleeping all the time. I feel weak and don't know what will become of me now as I no longer have any energy to fight anymore. I feel like I have been run over by a bus and then put through a mangle. I am in so much pain I feel as if someone is turning a machete right into my stomach! I am being sick again, up to ten times one after the other, with my legs springing up to my chest so that I have to kneel on the toilet. I feel like I am going to pass out. More blood, am I dying? What is happening to my body? I am falling apart but I must hold on to life as it is showing some signs of improvement. Surely I never got all this way off the streets to die in a fucking toilet in Rank Street, I continue to try and reassure myself.

"Are you all right in there, Katie?" asks Oliver my flatmate.

"No."

"Open the door Katie," says Oliver. "Oh my fucking God, you are losing blood! I will get a doctor here fast," and with that he leaves the bathroom.

At least he has called the doctor, I have been this sick in flats before and people have just left me to it.

When the doctor arrives he has a concerned look on his face.

"What have you eaten, Miss Brown?" he asks me.

"Toast, egg, chips, beans and a glass of milk," I say.

"My advice is don't eat bread and milk, you may be intolerant to these food groups due to having a weak system; I will refer you to a dietitian who will be able to help you work it out. I'll give you a prescription of some anti-sickness, anti-spasmodic, anti-diarrhoea and some Valium to help you sleep."

With that he is gone.

"How are you, Katie?" asks Oliver, concerned.

"I will be fine! At least for the first time in this life I have a wee bit of knowledge, thanks for helping me," I say.

"That's fine, really it is Katie, I am going to make some chamomile tea, do you want some?"

"That would be lovely, thanks!"

Oliver is making the tea, the drugs from the doctor are taking effect and the pain is releasing me. Ah! I can breathe again and have hope for the future because I will not eat wheat or dairy. I jump on anything, anything that will help me get out of this hellish way of living into a real existence. I'm finding this hard, real hard, but I must persist, I know it will be all right. My mindset is changing. I dare to relax my guard while Oliver is in the kitchen; I let myself feel safe for a moment, loved for a moment. A moment can last a lifetime.

The guard is back up but that little bit of love got in and it is growing alongside all the other bits of help or love that I have ever gotten; there is a glow, a chance. I must sleep now and tomorrow I must find that doctor and learn more.

Next day I go to the doctors and ask if I can see the doctor that was called out to me the night before.

"Sorry Miss Brown, he is a locum and you can't contact him or see him again," explains the doctor.

My heart sinks again. "What! Why? You must know who he is and I need to talk to him!"

"I'm sorry, Miss Brown, that's how the system works," the doctor responds.

"But he is the only one that has given me something to work with," I say.

"We will make an appointment for you with a dietitian, Miss Brown, they will be able to help you."

I have to go home and I am trying not to cry as I walk down the road to my house. I am on my own again. What the fuck am I supposed to do? I don't know!

In true Katie style I bounce back with a solution: I know, I will have a party! At least it will help the depression. I'll have a house-warming party. I ask my flatmates for permission and they are OK with it.

I'm not dead yet and I have a flat to party in; this is good. The game continues, I am a fighter and I will fight till I die if I have to, I can see no other way!

I call my mate and ask him to come and help me cook some wheat- and dairy-free party food.

The door goes and it is Gerome.

"Hello Katie," he says as he gives me a big hug, "what are we gonna cook?"

"I have dug out a recipe for a veggie meat loaf, if that makes any sense," I say, "with a secret ingredient!"

"What is that?" asks Gerome with a worried look on his face.

"Chilli, lots of it," I say.

"That will get the folks drinking," Gerome laughs.

"Ahh! Ahh!" I am screaming, running around the kitchen.

"What's wrong?" asks Gerome.

"I just blew my nose and have got chilli on it, ahh!"

My eyes are watering and I am going crazy, all the anger and frustration that I feel from my life has found a way out, I will blame the chilli! I start kicking the walls and put a hole in the wall behind the kitchen door. Gerome grabs me and tries to stop me.

"I told you, Katie, lay off the chilli, you need to give that snorting a rest." Gerome calms me down, reminding me that I rent that wall and not to damage it or I may lose it.

My flatmate is woken by all the commotion.

"What's going on?" asks Joe.

"It's all right, Katie just snorted a bit too much chilli!" laughs Gerome.

"I thought I was dreaming when I heard that being said," says Joe.

I tell Joe what happened and apologise for the wall with a promise to fix it.

"When are your guests coming?" asks Joe.

"They will start arriving about 8:30," I reply.

"I will just have a shower then, no more snorting chilli, OK?" he says as he heads to the bathroom.

The party is starting and the first to arrive is Jennifer. She lives across the main road from my flat.

"How's it going?" asks Jennifer as she walks in the door into the hall. "What smells nice?"

"That's the meat loaf with no meat," I reply.

"What?" asks Jennifer, puzzled.

"It's the veggie meat loaf," I say.

"Ehch! I won't be trying that, sounds fucking horrible," she says, "I will just crack open this bottle of wine instead. Where is your wine opener?"

"In the kitchen," I say.

"Hello Jennifer," says Gerome.

More guests start arriving and by now it's about 11:00 p.m. The party is buzzing and so are most of the guests. About 30 people have turned up and my mate is on the decks spinning the tecno tunes. Let's rock till we drop, which for me shouldn't be too long; I am still in pain but I drink the wine and take an E. I have an amazing ability to look like I am all good even when inside I am falling apart; old habits die hard or so they say.

Fuck knows when everybody leaves. I am well passed out even after all my efforts to stay awake. I wake up to a hell of a mess and a couple of mates, including Gerome, asleep in various places around the living room. My stomach is killing me so I take an anti-inflammatory, anti-diarrhoea, anti-sickness and a painkiller. The convulsions subside and a dozy daze of painkillers passes over me. Time is passing and I am a sick motherfucker but what am I gonna do? I can only acknowledge where I am lacking and that life is hard, sit with it then find a solution and hit back. Life is full of ups and downs, it's how you deal with the downs and enjoy the ups that counts. At least I am not homeless!

I have been in this house for a while, most of which I have spent in bed or being sick but my body has had enough struggles and is taking this opportunity to rest. I am so angry, frustrated and tired, I feel like there is a deep river of pain that could explode at any time.

My flat mate Oliver has offered to cook dinner for me tonight and Joe says he wants to tell us something. I wonder if he has bought me a present, ha!

Fat chance, just a wee indulgent thought. "Meat, potatoes and veg, ah!! What a good life," I say to Oliver as he serves the dinner.

"Hum! This is delicious, good effort," agrees Joe.

"Yeah, thanks Oliver," we say.

"Would anyone like a wee glass of wine?" asks Oliver.

"Yes that would be nice," me and Joe reply.

Oliver works in an off-licence downstairs so he often brings a good bottle of wine home.

"Well, enjoy your meal," says Oliver as if trying to cushion the news he has to tell us.

"What is it you want to tell us?" Joe asks Oliver.

I personally did not want to ask as news often means my life thrown into chaos and I couldn't cope with that just now.

"Well I was speaking to the landlord and he has decided to sell the flat so we will have to move out, we have two months," he responds.

There is silence. This news would have tainted the taste of the food if I wasn't so keen to enjoy this meal; things were about to get hard for me again and who knows if I will eat this well again in the next few months. I have to try and find rent and deposit for another flat and in Edinburgh this means at least £1,000. I will need to move when I can barely walk most days.

Fuck, what next? My mind is racing all over the place; I better get a grip on it and chill, enjoy my food then figure something out.

I go to my room feeling full but also with this sinking feeling like someone has just blown a hole in my safety raft and I am going down, all it takes is time! I wish I could have a home that is not taken away from me. Here we go again! The pain is rising and with the upset of the news coupled with the knowledge that I am really sick, I have to try and think of a plan of action to solve this problem. Sometimes I just wish I could give up and stop!

I tell Jennifer and she tells me I can live with her for a while, a couple of friends say they will help me move. I am too sick to lift and feel useless and embarrassed as I see all my friends moving my stuff for me to various places. Jennifer came and helped me walk across the road as recently I have taken to collapsing in the street. When it happens I am so scared, so vulnerable and hollow. I am also embarrassed as I am only 22 and feel so gnarly and fucked up.

Jennifer turns up at the bottom of the stairs of Rank Street. She has come to help me across the road to her flat. Thankfully it is not far, I just have to cross the main road and down a wee path between two buildings and we have arrived. It is a ground floor flat so I don't have to worry about climbing stairs.

Jennifer's house, another change! Jennifer is a wonderful woman. She is crazy but in a good way, she says I can share her bed as the sofa is the only other option and her son gets up for school in the morning. I can't sleep next to her as through the night as she intermittently stops breathing and I worry that she is dying; I don't sleep a wink and have to move to the sofa.

Jennifer is about 5'6" with mousy brown hair tailored around her face. She is of a slight build and she is a good-looking woman. I met her through her niece, me and her niece were friends from school. When I was 12 she told me that her auntie had been diagnosed with HIV and would I go to Edinburgh to go and see her.

Jennifer used to stay in a high-rise and when we arrived at her house she had three big bolts on the door as people kept kicking her door in when they found out she was HIV positive. That was then. Now Jennifer has full-blown AIDS and is only in her mid 30s. She has moved into town. She is a fighter, I have never seen anyone fight so hard to live and she seems to be winning just now. I love the way she mothers me, I love the way she cares and I feel loved in her home. She also guides me on what not to do. I have really lacked any kind of guidance in how to be since I was kicked out; it is hard when you just don't know!

"Right Katie, what is it that you are allowed to eat?" asks Jennifer.

"The doctor said no wheat and no dairy, rice cakes and such like," I reply.

"Well I know a wholefoods shop along the road, you just sit there and relax, I will go along and get some stuff, OK?"

"You don't have to do that, Jennifer."

"I know I don't, I want to," says Jennifer.

Off she goes to the shop, it makes me feel lovely sitting on the sofa with a quilt and a cup of tea. The gas fire is on and I am watching daytime TV feeling loved and cared for. It crosses my mind that my illness at least has brought me some help, I am now always looking for the silver lining!

"Hello! How are you my dear? I'm going to make you some lunch," says Jennifer, whipping past me heading towards the kitchen after her visit to the shops.

"Wow, I feel like a queen!" I say.

"No! I am the queen, you are my princess! Would you like some more tea with your lunch?"

"Yes please, Queen Jennifer," I reply.

There are sounds coming from the kitchen and I am busy rolling a joint. I see Jennifer coming out the kitchen into the living room with a bizarre look on her face.

"It smells good," I say, not showing the worry her face is causing me. She puts in front of me a plate with two pale white discs on it.

"Would you like some polystyrene circles with rice cheese and a wee bit of bacon? I feel like a bitch giving you that for your lunch, it looks awful, you will need a bucket of tea just to swallow it," she says.

"Thank you for trying, Jennifer, I appreciate it," I say as I crunch into a dry rice cracker with rice cheese. "This diet is weird; as everything has wheat or dairy or both in it, does nobody realise there are people who can't eat it?"

"It's bloody expensive as well," says Jennifer with a mouthful of soft bacon and cheese roll.

I have been a few weeks at Jennifer's and am starting to feel human a bit. We get on really well and it's nice to stay here as we have so much to talk about. It is amazing what a bit of love and care can do, without any fear of being kicked out. This is just what my body and soul need. My health is up and down. Some days I am OK, others I am sick and have diarrhoea and I have collapsed in the street a few times. I collapsed the other day and a hand came and helped me up and to my embarrassment it was a guy I used to fancy. He was so shocked to see me in this state. If any of them so-called friends from the dance and drug world had ever tried to keep in contact with me they would know what I am going through.

I am chilling in the living room. Billie Holiday is playing on the stereo and the bar fire is beating out heat just across the coffee table from me. I am swimming in the relaxation, my stomach is at the moment peaceful and I am 'stoned immaculate' on some good grass.

"Jennifer," I say.

"Yes love, what is it?"

"I have been invited to a party that Messenger sound systems are holding, the thing is I only know a couple of people that are going."

"And so?" asks Jennifer.

"Well, do you think I should go? I am going to get a lift but it is an outdoor event and I will have to sleep in a tent on my own."

"Yes, go! You only live once; if I didn't go out because I had to go alone I would hardly go out! Just go and you will meet some people and have a good time, it will do you good to get out for a while, where is it anyway?" she asks.

"Farvo woods," I reply.

"I think you should go, you are getting a lift so someone wants you there!"

"OK I will get it over with and I will go, thanks Jennifer."

"What are friends for, sweetheart?" she says.

I am packing for the festival and I am scared. I am weak but if I pack my anti-spasmodic, anti-sickness, anti-diarrhoea and painkiller medication I will at least not shit and puke everywhere while having a fucking painful stomach convulsion. I am told I am welcome but I still feel paranoid that they think I am a sad motherfucker and that they don't really like me but just feel sorry for me.

The words of my stepfather still ring in my head, "You are a crab! Nobody will be your friend unless they want something from you." I have had too many years of drugs and troubles and my mind is paranoid and tired of dealing with things. I can't rest, mentally I am holding on but I must keep going.

I arrive at the festival. As the car drives up the dirt track the sights become familiar to me; years ago when I lived in Farvo I remember this place. We get out of the car and greet Sam who is holding this party on his father's land. We are then led down the field towards some trees and as we arrive my smile becomes larger and larger as we reach a gate.

It is rusted iron and grand-looking and attached to a surrounding stone wall towering above us. Unable to resist the temptation, I open the gate; there is an eerie creaking sound, and we enter a garden that is like a mystery land, an enchanted garden. It has streams and little rocks to bounce over and is surrounded by the big stone wall that connects to a house far across the other side of the garden. I have returned to the Garden of Narnia after being granted the capacity to live, only this time it is filled with tents and a sound system. I am made to feel welcome and the set-up is one of the best I have seen yet and I have been to a few festivals.

In the dance music scene there is never any food but as this is a reggae event they have fires set up and they have killed one of Sam's mum's goats. There are four fires with big pots on them: one with lamb curry, one with rice, another with veggie curry. The music is playing a lovely relaxed reggae vibe and in amongst this I am a mental mess. In true Katie style I don't show that inside I am a paranoid wreck and am being horrible to myself, punishing myself, condemning myself, insulting myself, telling myself anytime now I would be used for something. I am ready to die, oh my God this is bad but I just can't stop the carousel of thoughts in my head. I go to my tent in case anyone can see my madness. I feel even weirder sitting inside this clammy bright tent. I am waiting for my mind to relax. I feel like I am missing being with a man and I feel deep inside me that if I am not being fucked then I am not loved and that means I am not good-looking or am not doing the right things. I am going crazy. The fear and paranoia is ripping through my brain, twisting and contorting my mind until all my thoughts are poisoned and my head is in pain.

Every now and then I step out of my sick mind and I appreciate the festival. I feel vulnerable; I have been through way too much hardness and abuse. I am now beginning to meet kind people, people who show they care, and I start to realise from my sweaty, tented cocoon that they don't want to rape me or feed me full of drugs and drink; chilled-out people who have respect for themselves, their bodies and their environment. This is all new for me and my defences are still high to hide my sick mind. I am suffering pain every day as it cuts through my stomach. The medicine only stops the symptoms, it is not changing my health, I am tired but still I carry on.

I don't quite know how to stop partying, it's all I have known for years. Don't know how and where to rest? It is strange that the safer I feel, the more I collapse.
I manage to pull myself together enough to talk to some people; I learn a lot and am beginning to see a new way to live. Maybe there is a chance!
I stay at the party for the weekend. I somehow manage to pack my tent and say goodbye to a few new friends and head to the car for my lift home.

I am back with Jennifer now and am glad to be back but am also glad I went; I must keep pushing my boundaries and hold on to my mind. If I don't socialise and make contact with other people and reality I will sink deeper into depression and then I lose all focus. After that it is even harder to come back.
Jennifer and I decide to go Dub Dept at Negations for the night. It is my first time wearing high heels and Jennifer has been told by the doctors to wear flat shoes. It is also her first time.

"Right, are we ready?" I say as I look into the mirror over the fireplace.
"Yes I think so," says Jennifer, casually checking herself in the mirror. We tentatively leave the living room with me holding on

to the walls then along the hall into the stairwell. It smells of piss out here as the jakies break in all the time to piss. We walk out the main door. Luckily Jennifer lives on the bottom floor.

As we try to walk up the street we are laughing at each other's attempts to adjust to the shoes we have on. We waddle and stumble halfway up the street.

"Jennifer!" I shout.

"What?"

"I can't walk, how do you walk in heels?" I ask her.

I am walking bowlegged by now like I have pissed myself.

"Fuck knows, I don't know how to walk in these flat shoes!" responds Jennifer as she walks like a duck with lead weights on her feet.

"We got to go back, it's no use," I say.

"I agree."

We looked a funny sight walking back over the cobbled streets of Edinburgh laughing.

We get home and quickly change.

"You ready?" I ask. "Yes and you?" responds Jennifer. "Let's go," we both say in unison.

We are able to walk high with intent all the way to the club in our sensible shoes and we dance all night to the reggae music till early hours in the morning.

Me staying with Jennifer is starting to put a strain on our relationship as she only has the sofa for me to sleep on. She is ill and the side-effects of her medication are an everyday battle. I am ill with my medication and its side effects, along with the lack of sleep. I can sense this before it becomes a problem; years on and off the streets, in and out of houses, you kinda get a sixth sense about these things even though Jennifer has said nothing. I watch her deal with living with AIDS and the pills she gets that keep her alive also have some evil side-effects. I watch her talk to me one minute then fall into a deep sleep the next. It is really hard for her and I am powerless to help her. I call a friend.

"Hi, how's it going?" asks Jewels.
"Pretty well but think I need to find somewhere else to stay as Jennifer is tired even though she won't admit it. Can you help me?" I ask him.
"I will ask my sister, you could maybe use our spare room for a while," he says.
So I thank Jennifer and move into Jewels's spare room for a while and then set about finding another deposit for a new flat, as even though this is a godsend it is a temporary arrangement. I end up being Jewels's girlfriend. I like him and he helps me so much that I kinda get confused between deep gratitude and love. Even though we are not meant for each other we have good times together.

My stomach has hit me again. I'm lying in Jewels's room listening to music wishing that I could astral project and leave my body and this pain behind when Jewels comes in.
"How are you?" he asks.
"I'm fucked, the pain is too much Jewels, I don't know what to do!" I cry.
"I have found a room that's coming up in my friend's house," he tells me.
"Brilliant, shall we go see her?" I ask.
"We will leave it a couple of days, rest for now, you can't even stand right now," he says.

CHAPTER 10
Pain and Beauty

I am now living at Jewels's friend's house in Turnberry. I have a small room but it is mine. I have set up housing benefit and am also applying for disability as my condition is getting worse. All I get given are painkillers and the other pills that I have already described. I rattle when I walk. I still go out to Dub Dept and hang out with Jennifer but I collapse in the street more these days, it embarrasses me. The dole has reduced my money because I have asked for disability. I now have £25 a week to live on. I feel like giving up but I can't, I have tried but you can't stop life just when you choose. I must somehow just get through this, how I don't know; I sometimes feel as if I am just existing at the moment. I do know life will change, nothing is permanent, all time is fluid.

There is a knock at the door.

"All right, how's it going"? It is Jewels.

"Ahh! You know, apart from pain every day, fine, and a pittance to buy all my wheat-free food!" I reply. "Thanks for getting me this house."

"It's cool, I just helped get the connection, you done the work, Katie! Do you fancy getting out the city now that your home is sorted?" asks Jewels.

"What you thinking?"

"I've got a sister lives in Gyle Peninsula up north," says Jewels.

"That's cool. Me and Gladis are swapping rooms around cos Mat's moving in this room. Can you help me pack my stuff in the cupboard and they could get on with it while I am away?" I ask him.

There is a policy that when one person moves out then we swap rooms, the last in gets the smallest room.

"OK shall we go then?" He helps put my newly unpacked possessions into a box.

"Yes we can, how do we get there? I don't have much money," I say to him.

"We can hitch to Inverness then we get picked up by Jacob, he will be doing their monthly food shop, we can get a boat over with them," Jewels tells me.

"A boat?" I enquire, puzzled.

"Yeh, you can only get in by boat or hike."

"I am glad I am getting the boat as I think the hike is well out of the question." Not in my emaciated state.

We pack my room in the cupboard and my stuff in my bag and off we go.

We are standing on the motorway hitching and I tell Jewels that I've never hitched before. "I do it all the time," he says.

"Do you think it will take us long?" I ask him.

"I don't know, you can never tell."

Time seems to be passing very slowly and I feel a bit stupid with my thumb out trying to stop cars that are going at least 70 mph past me. It starts to rain and I am very cold. I don't have much meat on me to keep in any warmth. I am still happy to be on an adventure though, and away from all the movement at the flat. Just then a lorry stops and up we climb. A few hitches later we are at the meeting point.

I am feeling very weak and don't like the hitching journey. We have arrived at the gas station where we will meet Jacob. While we are sitting waiting I ask Jewels if I can just buy a bus ticket back as I am too sick to deal with more fear and long waits at the side of the road. He agrees and tells me he will get it sorted before we leave. We have been waiting at the service station for a while now when Jewels's brother-in-law appears. They greet each other with love. I am unfortunately in a lot of pain and feeling cold. I am wondering if I have made the right decision as no one truly understands how painful my stomach is. I am so weak and yet I put on this hard exterior of someone who is fine, it is a trick that has served me well and it will not be easy to let go of.

We get in the minibus and there are about eight people. They also have bags of rice, wheat, oats, chocolate and stock for the month. This is all new for me. We drive another two hours or so before we arrive at the shore of a waterway and we get out of the van. I take a look and then a big deep breath in, ahh!! The fresh air is making me dizzy. Jewels comes up behind me and puts his arms around me giving me a big hug; I love this, it feels really good to have a supporting husband.

"Are you ready?" he asks.

"We gonna cross now?"

"Yep."

"OK I am ready," I reply.

We step into a little boat and we start across the water. I smile at Jewels as he is sat across from me and then I take in the amazing view of the hills and water. Wow, this is soul food! We arrive at the other side and as we step out the boat a massive shot of flames comes shooting up from an outboard engine on the shore. Two men who are fixing it drop it and jump back.

I look around and I pass some joke about a warm welcome. I find out that someone's boat had capsized earlier and they are trying to dry the engine out. Jewels is there again next to me, I like the way he cares. He is now saying hello to everyone and introduces them to me, he knows all the folks that stay here. I notice straight away how self-sufficient these people are and they are smiley and happy.

"You ready to walk along to Jezzy's?" Jewels asks (this is his sister).

"OK let's go, I will need to take it slow as my stomach is tiring me," I say.

"No problems. Our bags will be taken along on the quad bike then," he tells me.

"Thank you," I say.

The Gyle Peninsula is beautiful. I reach the top of the walkway to Jezzy's house and I look around at the hills and the views. My breath is taken away at the amazing rolling hills reaching as far as the eye can see. I see the waterway we have just come across. I am unable to see the other side on a far stretch of still waters. I look around where I am and I can see that the people here have built houses out of the ruins of old cottages that were left by the old settlers. They grow their own food and catch their own fish. There is only one flush toilet on the whole peninsula, only some houses have running water. A few days have passed and I am still unaware as to how I will shower myself. I am so desperate to get fresh and clean. I ask Jewels where I can go for a shower and he describes a waterfall along a path we had walked the day before collecting berries.

I decide I am afraid of my own stench and must go right away.

"I'm away for a shower," I say to Jewels.

"OK why don't you borrow this bike?" he offers.

I cycle to the nearest waterfall and I lay the bike down on the path and look up at the waterfall. It is a small climb away and looks lovely, lovely and cold! I must admit this rustic lifestyle is not for me, I enjoy the nature but some luxury would be good. I make the climb with care and am nervous as I am going to take my clothes off out in the open. I am also excited and worried and I am not looking forward to the cold. I am naked now and lay my clothes on a rock and step into the waterfall, my heart jumps and I let out a scream as the cold fresh water hits my body.

As the effects of the shock wear off I settle into having my shower. I look in front of me with my back to the rocks and my breath is again taken away as the land is beautiful and the sunlight is warm and soft on the rolling hills. It reminds me of an advert on TV for a shampoo called Timotei. I am exhilarated by washing in the fresh mountain water, my skin is tingling, my nipples are hard with a mixture of cold and excitement. I look down at my body, naked in the open surrounded by so much natural beauty. I see my stomach is concaved and my arms are thin, and for the first time I feel love for my body and I know now that I must cherish this body, care for this body. I silently cry a mixed cry – one of relief for being alive and one for all the abuse this frail body has taken. I spend some time just sitting on my towel letting the sun dry me off before putting my clothes back on.

I climb back down to my bike and set off home. There is a peace in my heart that I am not used to and a sense of what I have to do when I return home. Unfortunately on the way back I lose my balance and fall into a ditch; half of me now looks Timotei fresh and half is covered in mud and rotten leaves and smells like manure. I am not going back as I am exhausted after the cycle ride and I must rest a bit.

I see Jewels in the polytunnel tending to the sweet corn so I go in to say hello.

"Hello, how are you, there is a party on this afternoon, do you fancy going, what happened to you?" asks Jewels as I arrive.

"Cool, oh! I fell off my bike and fell in the quagmire, I will need to stand up wash to clean the rest of me," I reply back and ask him where the party is.

"It is around the other side of the Gyle," Jewels tells me.

"I will go and have a wee lie down then and get some power for tonight."

"OK, rest well, I will wake you near the time we are going," he says.

I have rested for a couple of hours and it is now time to get ready and follow Jewels to the water's edge. I am wondering why we are not walking over to the other side.

"We sailing to the party?" I ask in shock as this is all new to me.

"Yeh!" he says with one of his usual wide-eyed smiles.

"We are going to have a barbeque on the other side of the peninsula but we need to take a wee dip in nature's larder for the fish for the barbeque on the way," he tells me.

I don't understand and am puzzled as to what he means.

"Well here, does this explain it?" says Jewels as he hands me a fishing rod.

"Wow, this is all new experience to me!" I now get it!

We are sailing. "There's a shoal over the starboard bow," shouts Jimmy who is controlling the boat.

Jewels gets into action and baits up his fishing rod then drops the line over the right hand side of the boat.

"Do you want a shot, Katie?" he asks me.

"Yes please, I have limited knowledge but I have caught one fish before," I tell him, remembering my time with George.

Jewels moves over to me and hands me the rod with five hooks on it and sits behind me helping me to steady the rod. Feeling him close to me and caring for me is a heart-warming sensation.

"Just put it in the shoal," Jewels says as he helps me lower the line of hooks into the water.

"What, just here?" I ask.

"Yes that's cool."

"Then what?"

"Just wait."

I move the line in amongst the shoal and a minute later I feel a strong pull on the line. Luckily Jewels is behind me helping me as I try to pull up the line that is full with five mackerel.

"Wow, this is easy!" I am enjoying myself.

Jewels begins to take the fish off the line and place them in a bucket of water that is in the boat. We only put the line in a few more times and along with Jimmy's catch we are set for the party, fish for everyone!

We sail around the top of the peninsula and to the right of me I can see the hillside towering over us, it is lush and green. We steer more to the right and as we slowly sail around I see an inlet which we steer into. As we turn the corner we are greeted by other inhabitants of the peninsula.

"Hey how are you all?" asks Geraldine, a woman with a bright smile about 30 years old. She is wearing a colourful knitted jumper and brown cords and has a fine set of dreads. Geraldine has two children; her girl Indi is eight and is running around with pants on jumping into a loch with her older brother Josh who is similarly dressed.

"We are fine," says Jewels as he throws the rope to them to moor us.

"We got some fish for the barbecue," says Jimmy.

The barbecue is already hot and getting ready for the fish and there are people playing drums, violins, guitars and fiddles.

Wow! It is a sight I have never seen before and I love it. I walk through some rocks up from the shore line to where the party is happening. Wow, what a breathtaking scene! I look up and I am dwarfed by the hill in front of me and at the bottom of the hill, between me and it, is a still loch. I look around the loch; to my surprise I see loads of children joining Indi and her brother taking off their clothes and jumping in.

"Are you coming for a swim, Katie?" asks Jewels.

"You must be crazy, there is no way that I am coming in there, I will fall apart on impact, it is freezing."

"You will be fine," Jewels reassures me.

I don't care what he says I will not go in that water as I know how weak my body is right now. After all the activity today I must stay warm now and keep my movements reasonably slow. It is hard when people can't see the mess on the inside, when they can't see the pain that is tearing up my stomach.

We dance to the music, enjoying the day and the fresh air till dusk starts to fall over the hillside. It is rolling towards us as we are packing the boat up.

As we set off I realise that the mist has hit us.

"Wow Jewels! It is very spooky!" I am mesmerised.

"Yeh! Cool eh? We call it the Harr (Scots mist)," he explains.

The water is calm and still, the only ripples are the ones coming from the front of the boat slicing through the water. There is a two-inch gap between the water and the cover of the Harr. The air is filled so thick I can see only the moon's light breaking through it. I feel alone floating in the mist. It is a full moon tonight and through the mist I can see its round sphere so close to the water as if it could fall right in. I feel like I could be anywhere, I cannot even see Jewels, all I can feel is his strong hand holding me, this gives me the safety I need to enjoy this magical experience. Then out of the mist I hear a voice in the distance, "Ahoy there, ahoy there."

"Who is it, Jewels?" I ask.

"I think it is Graham; ahoy there," Jewels shouts back. The sounds come closer and, as if by magic, a boat pulls alongside ours out of the mist.

"Hello, how's it going?" asks Graham.

One of our passengers, after a quick conversation, climbs out of our boat and skips into Graham's and the boat disappears into the mist as if it were a ghost ship. I am again in the still calm with only the moonlight to guide me, it is a peaceful journey.

We arrive at the shore and unload our stuff, and then we wait for Graham's safe return. When are all safely on land Jewels leads me to the party's continuation in a newly built barn on Gyle Peninsula.

I love being here but we must return to Edinburgh and I must rest again. Even though these experiences have fed my soul and spirit, I am still sick and need to sleep and rest. When I am away from home my defence mechanisms kick in and I use energy to portray myself as feeling perfectly OK to others even when I feel like death warmed-up.

I am in need of a home, I have been adrift too much in my life; it is only another few days before we leave so I decide to enjoy my time here.

When I get back to Edinburgh things are changing between Jewels and I. There is a definite vibe between him and my flatmate Gladis.

My sickness is a major strain on Jewels and my health is deteriorating. Now that I am home it is as if it is now safe to collapse and my body does. I am now mostly bedridden, in pain every day and I can barely walk. I am angry and give a lot of my pain and stress to Jewels which is not fair but I lack any control. Every time I cough I shit myself. I am six stone and emaciated, I can't look after myself and I can't afford to eat wheat-free so I just don't eat because I don't know what to eat.

I am still waiting for my disability living allowance (DLA) so I am still on reduced benefit. I can only make it as far as the corner shop so I can't get much for my money.

I spend a year like this and I have deteriorated to such a bad state that I can no longer make it to the advice shop to sort my DLA. Jewels is now going out with Gladis in my home.

I am not meant for him so I will have to deal with it and they seem to be made for each other; even though I know this, it is twisting me up inside.

Gerome comes into my room with a poster saying, "I found this, look it says 'if you are being screwed by the dole write to this address'. What do you think, Katie?"

"Thanks Gerome, I will write to it and see what happens, anything is worth a chance," I tell him.

I write to the people at the address on the poster to ask for help. I get a reply that a woman is going to come round to help me. That's amazing, she is coming here because I can't get out of my bed as I am still very weak. I have a home help but she has told me I need to clean before she comes. 'What is the point in that?' I keep asking myself but at least she gets me wheat-free shopping. Also my other flatmates can't be bothered with cleaning before she comes.

The buzzer goes and it is the woman from the claimants.

"Hello, my name is Jasmine, I am from the claimants," she says as I let her in.

"Hi, thanks for coming to help me," I say as I go into my room and sit back into my bed. She proceeds to help me go through my files on the dole and breathes fresh air and knowledge through them. I feel like she is an angel who has come to help me as what she does helps me so much. I now know who to talk to; I contact my local MP and get him to help me.

I still find it hard to go in the kitchen and see Jewels and Gladis all lovey-dovey. I feel so unloved and in pain. I feel like I am living a useless existence. I am falling apart and it is taking all my effort to stay alive; the pain, the sickness and diarrhoea is too much, when will it stop?

My other flatmate has taken all my dope customers so I can't afford a smoke now and whenever I go in he puts his joint out. I feel so bad, I am very sad and I feel like a sick bitch. I hate the state I am in, I am at breaking point. I am starved of love. I see the flat walls so much and have barely any visitors. I feel like a waste of space, a fucked up waste of space.

I am so sad. I know I am hard to live with because I am fucked up but I feel like people would prefer that I just remain well hidden. It seems like society leaves children alone to fend for themselves at young ages and when they fuck up they just want to shove the product of this under the rug and don't want to deal with it. I am human and I have made wrong decisions; God help me, I did not know.

I start to feel so bad in this house. All sorts of thoughts go around in my head: I am not welcome, nobody wants to deal with me, why should they? They didn't fuck me up but I am erupting everywhere and they are in the fallout zone. So in true Katie style, I drag my sick ass out to Dub Dept to have a bit of life, Jennifer comes with me.

I have taken all my medication to prevent my insides falling out on the dance floor of the club and I hide my sickness well.
I meet a man called Paulo, I brush past his knee and there is this static feeling like sparks. I am so sad within and I am just looking for someone to love me. I am six stone and by rights should be in my bed. I invite him to spend the night with me. He does and we have sex; it is a non-event, I don't want it as he is drunk and I am sick. All I want is to be cuddled for a night. So I let him have sex with me then we cuddle all night.

A couple of days later Jasmine came around to see me. I am happy to have a visitor. "You can come and stay at my home if you want, Katie; my flatmates have said it is OK. We have a cupboard under the stairs that has a window; you are welcome to stay there till you get your money and get your own flat," she tells me.

So I am moving again; I get rid of most of my possessions and move into a cupboard under the stairs. It is a strange sensation when people run up the stairs – it is like they are running up my ribs. I am so thankful to be leaving that flat, I feel like I belong in a cupboard anyway. I will stay here till I get my backdated DLA.

CHAPTER 11

Love and Light

I have given up my possessions, I have just what is in the rucksack on my back. I walk into Jasmine's and ring her buzzer. "Come in," she says.

"Thank you," I say, panting after dragging myself and my bag up four massive flights of stairs. As I am climbing up them I see above me bright sunlight coming through the stairwell sky light, it is so lovely and warm on the stairs on this sunny day that it makes me feel good. I am worn out and am having to take deep breaths now. The door opens and there stands Jasmine. She takes my bag and shows me in. I walk to the right along the hall and she motions to a room on the left at the end of it. I walk in. It is the kitchen containing a big massive heavy wooden table surrounded by chairs, on which I take a well-needed sit down. Jasmine has three cats and they all come and start circling me and checking me out. I look to my left and my breath is taken away by the view I see. It is a panoramic view of Edinburgh, all the famous sights: Arthur's seat, Carlton Hill, the Pentlands and the castle – wow!

"This is Wale," Jasmine introduces me to one of the flatmates.
"Hey, I'm Katie, thank you for letting me stay here," I say.
"That's cool, you are welcome," replies Wale.
"Here, let me show you to your room," says Jasmine and leads me back along the hall and as we come to the front door she points opposite it to a door tucked under the stairs. She opens it and I am half expecting a family of Borrowers to come out of the room. I look inside and assess my new home. It is smaller than a single bed, with a window straight opposite the door and tucked under the stairs on my left is a pile of mattresses.

It is small but nice, kinda like a deluxe cupboard. "Thank you,"

I thank Jasmine.

"You are welcome, Katie, I am glad I could help you," she replies.

The next day I write to the DLA to change my address to a temporary c/o address at Jasmine's. I am hoping I will hear soon when I am going to get my backdated money, assuming my appeal will won. It has been two years since I have been fighting for this help from the dole.

Jasmine is always busy with lovely people; our other flatmate is a DJ and has an enormous record collection; Wale has a studio where he produces music.

Time passes and I am doing everything I can to improve my health and situation; I love the break the cupboard has given me but I would love my own flat to recover in. I have managed to start contacting my mum now as her and George have broken up. I would love somewhere I could be proud of. I feel I am always on borrowed time in these temporary places and it is a strain on my health. I want to get homeopathic help but I can't afford it as I am still on reduced money as I am still waiting for the DLA's decision.

I turn to herbalist treatment as they have a free clinic on a Wednesday at Naipers. I have to pay for the medicine though, but I will just have to manage.

Today I have to go and see my herbalist so I drag my sick-ass body out of the house and down the massive flight of stairs. I come out the stairwell and turn right down the street to the bus stop. The weather is warming up but there is still a chill in the air; I wrap my collar around my neck as I feel the cold air hit the back of my throat. I have to wait for a bus so I take a seat in the bus stop and as I am sitting there I notice a woman coming into the bus stop.

"It's still a bit chilly isn't it?" she says.

"Yes," I say.

As I am sitting there I can see leaflets in her hand saying 'healing'. I feel myself starting to lean towards the leaflets, I see the words 'Reiki Healing'.

As I lean closer and closer to the woman she begins to notice me so I ask her, "What's that?"

"It is a form of hands-on healing, it comes from ancient Japan," she says.

"What is Reiki?" I ask.

"Reiki means light force, it is calming, relaxing and healing," explains the woman.

"I need some healing but am unemployed, do you do concessions?" I ask. "Yes, I am sure we could come to some arrangement, here why don't you have a leaflet and give me a call. My name is Jessy."

"I will be in touch," I promise as I climb into the bus; I go flying up the bus as the driver does not wait till I am seated. I am young and shouldn't be so sick and people don't give you any room for your disabilities, especially if they can not outwardly see them. I go to the herbalist and get some medicine before heading straight back to the cupboard to sleep. The journey has taken it out of me.

When I wake up and go to have some dinner, Jasmine is there so I tell her about the meeting at the bus stop and about my hope that this Reiki will help me heal and become healthy again.

"When your money comes through you could go, Wale's mum

is a Reiki Master," she tells me.

"I would like to get in touch with her if possible," I say.

"I'm sure that will be fine," says Jasmine and we enjoy the rest of our dinner. I bid my farewells and go back to bed. I am so tired all the time, I kinda think it is because of all the nights I have spent awake or sleeping in danger. I now have a safe place to sleep and my body wants to do nothing else.

I awake to the sound of the buzzer at about 1:00 p.m. on Saturday. "That is Paulo at the door," says Jasmine. She does not much like Paulo but any love is good for me and what little he gives me is better than nothing in my eyes. Anyway I have enough unspent love for the both of us which I am sure will be my downfall.

"Hello," I say.

"Ola," replies Paulo.

"Come into my room," and I lead him into my cupboard space. We fuck the rest of the day and some of the night and we barely come up for air. He has many bruises on his back and head from the stairs; when life is hard it all feels bearable when you get a good fuck. I have stopped taking drugs; as a rule I only smoke dope and wonder if this is my new addiction. I love pushing that hard cock into me and watching his studious ass bumping up and down as he gives it to me tight. Is this love?

We both have a joint and then pass out on the pile of single mattresses that is my bed under the stairs; we wake up with our faces squashed together due to the incessant rolling effect of the mattress pile. I don't mind as I love having another body close to mine, hugs are great!

It is Monday morning now. Paulo went home yesterday and I am still eagerly waiting for the post and the letter from the DLA tribunal. I walk to the front door, half excited, half nervous, in case it doesn't come. There, in amongst the pile of letters, I see a brown envelope; I know is from the dole. I tentatively pick it up and go straight to Jasmine's room; I knock quietly on her door not wanting to wake her but hoping that I will.

"Come in," she says sleepily.

As I walk in across from the door there is a mattress on the floor. She is all tucked up although it is quite bright in her room. I look to my left where I see a thin piece of white cotton hanging across the window. As my eyes scan across the room back to Jasmine I see books lined up all along the skirting boards, books of knowledge.

"I am sorry to wake you! I hate waking people up," I say, "I just couldn't wait, I have a letter from the DLA."

"That's all right," Jasmine says as she stretches in her feline-like manner, "come and sit down." She gestures towards the bottom of the bed as her entourage of cats leave the bed. I open the letter.

"Yee ha!" I shout out in a muffled shout.

"Did you get it?" asks Jasmine.

"Yes I did!" I say as tears fill my eyes, tears of relief; two years of fighting and struggling because of one doctor's view of me. I remember the doctor's comment that caused this problem was 'strange girl, thin legs but otherwise normal, she likes to read and draw all day'. He didn't add this was because I was bedridden and trying to prevent brain damage from boredom. This was the end of that fight and I am so relieved.

"How much did you get?" asks Jasmine.

"£4,000."

"Great, shall we have a tea?" asks Jasmine.

"Yeh! I will go and put the kettle on." I run off to do so.

I leave Jasmine's room and go across the hall to the kitchen and put the kettle on. My mind is buzzing with what to do, I have never had so much money in cash before. I have already been talking with my friend Morgan about going to Portugal as I want to find out more about Paulo's culture and the country in which he was brought up. For some reason he refuses to come with me and refuses to let me know where his family live. What can I do? Nothing!

I call Morgan.

"I got the money," I tell him.

"Excellent, you up for going to Portugal then?" she asks.

We both agreed the next month we would go to Portugal and then we set about getting our tickets.

I spend some of my money on an overlocker sewing machine to do some dressmaking to try to earn some extra money or at least to make some much needed clothes. When I get home with the overlocker I find it too hard to understand all the instructions. I express this to Jasmine and she tells me to speak to Wale as she is sure his mother sews. I get her number off Wale and give her call and she tells me she wouldn't mind helping me and that she will be free in a couple of weeks. The next mission is to get the Reiki treatment on the go so I call the lady I had met at the bus stop and we arrange an appointment. I also know I must use this money to get myself a home so I go looking for a flat. Luckily one comes up just around the corner from Jasmine and with the extra money I am getting from the disability I will be able to rent on my own. I feel this is necessary as I need to go through a healing period; it is coming, I can feel it, I am ready. I decide to give my mum a call and tell her the news, I hope she will come and visit me when I get a new place. It is so hard to move forward with all this past hanging around my neck.

I tell the guy who owns the flat I am a fashion designer. I get some references from a friend and the flat is mine. I move in within two weeks' time.

I am off to see the Reiki Master for some healing, my body is tired and it has used loads of precious energy doing all this flat organising. I must drag my ass down the road to her house. She doesn't live far enough away for a bus but the walk is extremely hard for me in my depleted state. I arrive at her house and lean on the wall for a few breaths; that was another use of pure willpower. I knock on the door and wait; there is no answer. I wait for ten minutes, not wanting to go home without having a healing. I am nearly crying as I was so looking forward to the healing and the bitch is not in. Why she gonna leave me here? I am too sick for this. There is nothing I can do but go home so I start the arduous walk home where on my return I slump on my bed and cry. The pain is cutting in and all the effort from the previous days is now hitting me. I take a painkiller and fall asleep.

I move into my new flat; I look around me with relief that finally I have a flat that I can spend time on my own fixing myself.

I have got a phone fitted first as this is very important. Communication is the key to not going crazy, for me anyway, and the Samaritans are really helping keep me from falling over the edge.

I am chilling, looking around the living room from my sofa and the phone rings. I smile as I lift the receiver, my first call!

"Ola, it's Paulo. How is your new flat?"

"It is lovely, when you coming to see it?" I ask him.

"I will come over tomorrow, OK?" he says.

"Yeh, this will be fine," I say. Well, my first call from my boyfriend! I take stock; I have a flat and a boyfriend, I am sure this is life getting better.

The phone rings again as soon as I put it down. The excitement is too much, who could this be, I wonder?

"Hello Katie, it is Kelis, I am Wale's mum, he said you needed help with your overlocker."

"Yes I do, this would be great," I reply.

"Would I be able to come about six tomorrow night?" she asks me.

"Yeh, this would be great, see you tomorrow."

I am so happy; I have a new house and people actually phone me so this is all good. I will try and make sense of unpacking these boxes and make this my home. I am so used to moving that I make a home really fast as I want to enjoy it as much as I can. Who knows how long this will last. I put on the music and start to unpack and whilst unpacking I note that on average I have moved every two months since I was 15; I am now 23. This is a bit of a tiring hobby, I must find a new one. I hang on to so much crap in the vain hope that I will have something familiar in the houses I move to. Unpacking done and I am knackered; my house is looking like Katie's house so I will go and sleep. Tomorrow is another day.

I awake to the buzzer going and as I turn over in my bed I notice that it is dark outside; I am confused, I must have slept all day. The buzzer is going again. "All right I am coming," I yell.

I answer the buzzer and it is Paulo.

"Ola."

"Come in, welcome to my new home," I say, gesturing to him to enter the hall. "What time is it, babes?" I ask him.

"It's 5:00 p.m.," he replies.

"Shit! I have Wale's mum coming around in an hour, I must go shower."

"Do you want me to cook some food?" asks Paulo.

"That would be brilliant, here let me show you around," and I take him on the tour. I walk along the hall and signal to the left. "And here I have the box room," I say as I show him the room with no window. It is small and dark but maybe I will make it into a work room or cupboard, who knows just now? I continue the tour. Around to the right is my bedroom; it is very green but a nice size and full of boxes. My bed is just as you walk in across from the door. To the left of that is the window with my brand new overlocker on top of my old Singer sewing machine. Then past the small bathroom that is in between the living room and the bedroom. It is small but warm with the window overlooking half the road as it is a basement flat. In the corner of the living room there is a cupboard which is called a kitchen. I am amazed what landlords can get away with calling a kitchen. As you walk in the glass box you can only fit you in it, and when you turn around you can touch each side. Well at least I am not homeless.

"So that is my tour de Katie's, I must now shower; help yourself to the food but I must warn you I am on a weird-ass diet – no wheat or dairy, OK?" I remind him.

I am out the shower now and I can smell the dinner cooking in my new house.

The buzzer is going again, oh! I am a popular girl tonight, it must be Kelis.

"Hello Kelis, come in," I say.

I show her to my overlocker.

"Well, how is your new house, Katie?" says Kelis.

"Well, I am enjoying it a lot, Paulo is cooking me a nice dinner so it is mighty fine; how are you Kelis?" I ask her.

"I am good, I have just set up a Reiki practice at the end of the street, actually; I have been painting tonight, that's why I could come."

I told Kelis about my experience with the last Reiki person.

"You should come to see me, I will be able to offer you concessions because you are unemployed," she tells me.

We make an appointment for the end of the week as I am off to Portugal soon for my first holiday abroad. I really want to start my healing before I go and get some rest.

"Thanks for helping me with my overlocker and I will see you soon," I say as she leaves. Dinner is ready.

Life is good, I feel happy as I eat my dinner prepared by my man and I am looking forward to going to Portugal.

The week soon passes and I have been excited all week about getting my Reiki treatment. I don't need to go far, it is just at the end of the road. As I walk towards the Reiki studio I have a sense in my heart that life will keep getting better. Soon I arrive and Kelis opens the door, she shows me into a candlelit room that smells like heaven. Across the room is a massage table and there is soft music playing in the background.

"How are you, Katie?" Kelis asks.

"I am OK."

She passes me a document to fill in with my details and explains what she will do during the healing session. I climb on to the table with all my clothes on and she gently covers me with a soft blanket.

The treatment lasts for one hour as Kelis lays her hands over the various energy centres on my body; she explains them as 'Chakras'. I feel as if I am drinking in love and light, I keep peeking as I am intrigued as to what she is doing. This is all new to me, after the treatment I am deeply relaxed. Kelis advises me to keep coming back regularly for a while, she also says, "You kept peeking, why was that?" "I was interested in what you were doing, I have never felt such peace before," I reply.
After I come back from Portugal I will book in for some more treatments.
"I am running a Reiki 1 attunement course; if you are interested in becoming attuned you will be able to treat yourself whenever you need to," she explains.
"OK, I think this would be a good option for me," I reply.
I say goodbye and go home for the most peaceful sleep I can ever remember having.

CHAPTER 12

is it? Was it? Could it?

I am confused. Paulo is sometimes very loving and sometimes not. He is always there during the week at nights, and at weekends he is unavailable. I am not sure what is going on with me and him. Maybe a holiday together would make it better?

"Paulo, why don't we go to the Highlands for a wee break together?" I ask him one day.
"No, you're all right, I don't want to," is his response.
"But we are not getting on and maybe a wee break together would be nice, or shall we spend some time doing things of interest? We spend a lot of time doing things that interest you and never things that I am interested in. Please come."
"Got no money", he says.
"I will pay; I will hire a car if you drive it," I suggest.
"No, where would we stay?"
"We could stay in a B & B."
"I don't want to! Go yourself."
"Thank you," I say sarcastically.

After a week of crying and begging him and him laughing and gloating at me, finally he decides to come with me. I pay for everything, of course. It is a nice weekend and the Highlands are beautiful: the rolling hillsides, the lochs so still as if they are a mirror. We stay in B & Bs, we make fires and cook on them, we get lost in valleys. I flourish being in the outdoors and I love being in love with this man. I am so attracted to him that I can't keep my hands off him. We pull up the car by a loch side late one evening and I set about rolling a joint. It is so peaceful here away from the city; I am enjoying the smooth stone the dope provides and the warm arms of my man. Paulo tells me he has fallen in love with me. Finally he loves me but I find it hard to get to the real Paulo a lot of the time. I know he is in there somewhere. Out here he lets his guard down and drops all pretences. This is the man I love, I feel like I don't want to ever go back, I wish to stay in this moment forever.

But alas the dream ends, the rental car time runs out and so does my money, so we are now back in my flat in Edinburgh.

The day after we get back my mate Liam comes to see me; he asks if I am doing anything at the weekend, I tell him I have no plans.

"We're getting a van together and going to Manchester. Paul and Mick are opening a new club. Are you coming?"

"Yeh, that will be cool. Can I bring Jennifer along with me?" I ask him.

"Yeh, that's cool man, we'll meet Friday 6:00 p.m., at my house," he says.

"OK! I'll be there," I confirm.

I go to Liam's at six o'clock with Jennifer to join the party crew from where we go to Manchester and we party hard all weekend, taking copious amounts of drugs and dancing all night and partying in the day. What a laugh! I come back and personally I am finding it hard to have fun on drugs anymore. I just get paranoid, my mind is so tired. I have had enough of this, but I do not know any other way. I am looking forward to seeing Paulo, he's coming round tomorrow.

"How did it go with Liam?" asks Paulo the next day.

"Aye, it was fun. You should have seen Dave and his crazy monster outfit," I tell him. "You look tired, shall I cook something?" asks Paulo.

"Yeh, that would be lovely, thanks. I shall have a bath."

We're getting on good again, I love this man, it is nice to see him as I have missed him while I was away. It is amazing what a good break does for you. Paulo and I are staying in for a couple of days together, eating and fucking; it's an easy existence and the fantasy ends when Paulo has to go and hook up with some friends.

Two weeks have passed now, I have not seen much of Paulo and my period is late. I think I may be pregnant. I know when it happened and I feel different. I get a Clear Blue test and it reveals what I already know, so I contact Paulo and ask him to come round as I need to tell him something.

"Paulo, we are pregnant," I say.

"Are you sure?" he asks.

"Yeh, my breasts are larger and wobbly, I am also late for my period and I have had a test; you remember a couple of weeks ago don't you?" I say.

He looks at me with a glint in his eyes. We both remember the night of hot passion and we knew we had pushed the boundaries too far, but I would not take another morning-after pill as they were so bad for my system. Strangely enough, he never seemed to be there when I went through the debilitating side-effects of dizziness and stomach cramps, so bad that I am unable to walk. He turns around to me and says, "Have an abortion; don't have a child with me."

"Why not? I love you!" I respond.

"I am not the kind of person to have a child with. It will do you no good," he continues.

Here I go again! I have a feeling he is saying this because of his lack of confidence in himself and his depression.

"I can't have an abortion, I have never had one and never want to and I love you. This child will be born with love and of love," I tell him.

Any further complaining from him I ignore as I decide I will keep the baby. I leave the room after telling him he will be a dad.

"Yes!" I say under my breath with excitement as I enter the hall. I thought I was too sick to have conceived and think it must be a blessing, maybe the only chance I will ever have. I feel I should take it and have this baby and think about being healthy, eat nice food, exercise, meditation, Reiki etc.

Just then Jennifer phones me. "There's another party in Manchester this weekend. You've got to come."

"I can't," I tell her.

"Come on Katie, why not?"

"I am pregnant."

"What? Wow! Are you? I am so happy for you. Are you happy?" she asks me. "Yeh, very happy, but there will be no talk of parties," I tell her. I feel secretly relieved as I want to stop taking drugs anyway.

"You can still come, you just don't need to take anything," she says.

"You've got no chance, I'm not going."

Liam comes to see me soon after that.

"There's a party in Manchester at the weekend, are you coming?"

"No, I'm sorry I can't, I'm pregnant."

"Wow, are you happy?" he asks.

"Yes I am, but no more drugs!" I tell him.

After he leaves I am relieved, I do not want any more of that. I now have the perfect reason to be good, my child depends on it. I phone my nan, I need to reach out to someone, someone who I know I have so much respect for. We have always kept a line of communication open: the odd letter, the odd phone call. "Nan can I come and stay with you? I have to give up smoking!" "Yes, you can come," she says.

I know that living there I would feel guilty every time I smoke and that I would never want to disappoint my nan and granddad. Also they would smell a mile away if I even have a quick ciggy down the beach. I give up smoking, cold turkey for three weeks. I will never go back to fags again.

I am back home now and sad because Paulo I and are not getting on. He is only interested in me serving his needs, and I am feeling neglected. I am weary now, I literally had to beg him to stay with me tonight. The phone rings. "Morada is having a party tonight, are you coming?" asks Paulo's brother on the other end of the phone. Paulo looks at me, I look at him. He knows I want to stay in tonight.

"I'll call you back in a minute," Paulo says to his brother and hangs up.

"Shall we go to this party?" asks Paulo.

"I just want to chill in. You said we could chill in together," I remind him.

"Yeh, it will just be for a little bit. We'll just go for an hour, just one drink," he says.

He eventually verbally beats me down, I find myself saying, "OK, just for an hour." The words are sickening me as they fall out my mouth and my heart has sunk. I will not get to chill, I know that I will have to get into survival mode.

"You promise me that when I need to come home, you will come with me?" I ask. "Yes, that's fine," he replies with his jacket already on.

I am five months pregnant now. It is becoming a chore to carry myself.

"You promise me if I need you to come home you will," I say again, worried due to past experience.

"Yeh, yeh, don't worry," reassures Paulo.

"Ola!" Paulo says to his brother and sister. "How are you?"

"Fine!" they say. "Come and sit down, have a glass of whisky, join the party," says Joel, Paulo's brother, as he motions towards a table in the middle of a hall packed with little kilted children running around chasing little girls in bridesmaid dresses. The party is in a church and the smell of curry and pakora fills the room. I sit down; as I look up I can see far at the other side of the room the head table where the wedding party are sat. I make a conscious decision to enjoy my time here as I will only be here a few hours and I hate not to enjoy things that I go to. I always feel stupid if I am somewhere and I am not enjoying it; why be there, eh? Time goes on and a couple of hours pass.

"Paulo, can we go home now?" I ask him.

"Em, my sister is talking about going to Messenger at the Bongo club. I want to go along to that, it's not far," Paulo says.

"Paulo I need to go home, I am carrying your child, it is heavy. I want to go home and I would love it if you would want to come with me rather than leave me five months pregnant walking the streets alone to get home," I stress.

"Oh come on, you are always going on at me, come on. You

have to come, it will be fun, you will see," is the response from Paulo.

Before I know it I find myself walking uphill along Regents Terrace, down the steep, dark stairs that lead down through the hill, which is a short cut along to the Bongo Club. I slip on rotten leaves and crisp packets and used condoms. Lucky I don't fall, no thanks to this so-called man who is supposed to love me. What is love? I am not sure I know what love is, I am so needy that I allow Paulo to do this to me. Why have I not just gone home already?

I arrive at the Bongo Club and there is a queue. After waiting some time at the stairs to get in we enter. As soon as I get in Paulo loses me and the heat and humidity of hundreds of people dancing and sweating hits me and constricts my breathing. There is loads of dry ice and it is dark, I can hardly see anyone. Even the chill-out is packed. I feel as if people are staring at me, wondering why I am here pregnant. I try to lose myself in the dark, the dancing, making the most of it as I always do – dancing, enjoying the music. It is a tiring effort as the pain in my heart is heavy. I am carrying this man's child and still my needs and emotions mean nothing. Suddenly it feels like my womb has dropped, and the safety of the dance which I have relied on for so many years has been broken. It is no longer available to me, I can no longer hide here.
It is my first child, I do not know if this is normal.

I find Paulo, drinking. "Come on Paulo, I need to go now. You said you would come," I insist.
"Oh, but stop hassling me! After this drink I will come."

He drinks the drink. I come back. He still won't come, downing more drinks and dancing with young unpregnant women and looking at me with an evil eye. I am slowly crumbling, why I am here? I don't know; why can't I bring myself to leave? Am I scared of leaving because if I do this means something is very wrong with my relationship and I would have to face it? Can I face it if I do? He may leave me pregnant and alone. I have no family support and I have no strength to leave and face all this. Finally, at 2:30 in the morning with much persuasion, he leaves.

He has my key in his pocket as my pregnancy dress does not have any pockets. We will have to walk all the way home as there are never any taxis in Edinburgh at the weekend. As we are walking home I turn around and notice he is not there. I feel lost standing at the top of Leith Walk, five months pregnant, on my own, no keys to get in my house. Where the fuck is he? I sit there, God knows how long, wanting to cry but not wanting to show any weakness in the street, feeling fucking stupid. "Why, why? Why did I believe he would come?" I repeatedly say to myself. Why didn't I just go home earlier and save myself the hassle?

In my heart I know why: I want him to want to protect me and be with me; I want to be near him, I want to be loved. I hate myself for this weakness, the weakness of wanting to be loved.

"Ola Katie, how are you doing? What are you doing here? Where did you go?" asks Paulo in a stupid, drunk, nonchalant way when he finally turns up.

"Where the fuck have you been? You just left me standing at the top of Leith Walk on a Saturday night," I yell.

"I just needed some fags, then I bumped into a couple of my

mates, and … you know," he says.

"All right! I can see you really care, just fucking take me home," I say, tired.

As the days pass I become more depressed; I am having this man's child and he has no care for me or respect. He is so selfish.

Gerome comes round to visit me one day.

"John's flat is going to be empty soon, I thought I would tell you," he says.

I arrange with John to go and look at his flat and Gerome comes with me.

"Hello John."

"All right Katie, how's it going?" he asks.

"Just keen to see this flat," I tell him.

"Well let's go in, I must warn you the last tenant didn't leave it in a good state," he warns.

As we open the door we are greeted by a dirty red carpet that is not even attached to the floor, and dirty walls with the wallpaper hanging off them. I walk into the first bedroom and I see the thin grey carpet with stains all over it and dark purple walls. Across the room out the window I see there is a really nice view. I can see the whole Edinburgh panorama: the castle, the mound, Arthur's seat and behind them Pentlands – this view is amazing.

"I'm sorry about the mess," he says.

"To tell you the truth I will just be happy to have a flat for a decent amount of time, is two years cool to start?" I ask.

"Yeh, we'll call it two years then see," he agrees.

"There will need to be some changes to the interior," I tell him as I enter the kitchen/living room. It has still got mouldy pans on the cooker and the ceramic fireplace is badly chipped.

"That's cool," he says.

"It's a deal then," I say.

So I start a new life in my new flat, I am eight months pregnant now and happy to have this space to raise a family in. I am also happy to know my landlord and to have a secure lease with plenty of room to grow. Maybe things will be better with Paulo now.

It is three weeks before the birth of my child. I have been getting regular Reiki and as I now have my Reiki 2 certificate I have been treating myself and my baby. Paulo's mum Barbara has come to help us out and feed me. She is amazing, she looks after me as I am preparing to have my baby at home. It never occurred to me to go to hospital; giving birth is a natural process. I am sure it will be fine, I have suffered pain before. I prepare my house. I order the water pool. Paulo wants me to go to hospital and the nurses are telling me to go to hospital; Paulo's mother is telling me it isn't safe and that I should go to hospital. I am stubborn and I flatly refuse. A few days before my son is due I invite the people who are to be present at the birth: my mum, Paulo and his mother and my friend Morgan come round. We are having dinner and a dummy run of setting up and filling the pool, and as Barbara is sleeping in the room where I am to give birth this will mean removing the bed and setting up the pool when labour starts.

We do well and everyone knows what they are to do on the day. On the day my son is due I feel twinges in my body as I am sat in a yoga position meditating and sending Reiki to him asking him to come, so I know he is coming.

I tell Paulo's mum, "Today the baby is coming."

"No, no, don't be silly, they never come on time," Barbara says back.

I know it is coming, I have sent a Reiki meditation and called my baby, "Come on child, it is time," I have said, "it is time to come." I call the nurse to come and check my dilation. "You are in the first stage of labour," she says. I am so happy to have it confirmed.

I proudly walk through to my living room and announce to Paulo and Barbara the news. I then call my friend who is going to administer homeopathic medicine if I need it and my mother who will be there. Barbara passes me some lovely Portuguese prawns and tells me I will need my strength. My mother says she will be there in three hours. When the pool is set up I climb in and enjoy the pain relief it gives me as I have been in labour for several hours now.

Morgan passes me water laced with St Johns Wort for energy and intermittent arnica for stress and bruising. My mum climbs into the pool with me. She is amazing and tells me to breathe. I shout; I have changed my mind, this is too painful. I feel my body change rhythm from an opening sensation to an immense pushing feeling that rocks my whole body; my child will be here soon. All I can hear is my mum's voice saying, "Just breathe, you are doing well."

My son Jackson is born into my mother's hands after eight hours of labour. I tore my vagina five ways and have to be stitched up with no pain relief but I am so numb that I didn't feel this until days after when the stitches were taken out. The birth has gone extremely well. I have given birth into my mum's hands in the water pool, in the room that is to be my son's room. I lie there after giving birth in my bed feeling like I have been run over by a truck. It is two weeks before I can walk again.

I have my first expedition out to the shops, with Paulo. "Come on lazy, are you coming to the shops?" he says.

"Yeh, I think I will, I will try." I am walking like I have shat myself, but I can't close my legs properly because of the wounds around my vagina. I put on a long skirt to cover the wounds and my feelings before I put on a jacket.

"Right I am ready," I say to Paulo.

"You're not going looking like that, are you? You look a state," he says to me.

"Thanks Paulo, that will give me a lot more confidence for going out," I retort back. We are walking down the street and walk past a clothes shop.

"Why don't we go in and have a look for some new clothes for you," Paulo says. I smile, my heart lightened. "Oh, that's nice," I say, "yeh, let's do it." I walk into the shop, I turn around and he is standing at the door of the shop.

"Why aren't you coming in, Paulo?"

"I didn't say I was gonna go with you." My heart sinks again; it is that feeling, that emotional up and down, up and down, until I don't know where I am.

I try and get over it. I try and make myself happy, we go and get the photos I have given in to be developed and come back home. I am very sad; the only thing that brings me joy is Jackson.

As time goes on I realise that I am with Jackson on my own

a lot of the time. Paulo comes in from work, he watches Jerry Springer, he gets drunk and persuades me to do things that he likes. In the end my son is cowering in his arms at the sight of the nerds on Jerry Springer as the only way he can get a cuddle is when he sits by his dad. It hasn't occurred to his dad to turn off the TV and pay attention to his son. He lives in my home, pays no rent, no heating or electricity; he gives me money towards it at the weekend and then promptly takes me to the shops to spend it on wine and food. He doesn't seem to mind spending on my credit card either.

Most of the pictures I have of days out are of me and Jackson; Paolo is not in them. I am repeatedly getting thrush and tonsillitis; the stress is getting too much for me. I love this man, but I don't know what is going on. We are going to Portugal together next week; I am hoping a holiday will be good for us, where we can spend some time together as a family, on my credit of course. He can't get credit at the moment as he is not from here. In fact I cover most costs; he is a freeloader, how the hell did I get here? I am getting deeper and deeper into debt and he doesn't even see that it has anything to do with him!

We arrive in Portugal and Paulo is showing Jackson off to his relatives. Paulo says he will take me to visit some of his friends. He introduces me to some of his friends then disappears to the kitchen, leaving me with Jackson in the living room with his friend's wife. I have never met her before and she doesn't even speak my language. She looks at me and says hello then she walks across the tiled living room past the dining table to a big dresser cabinet to the right of the window where she reaches inside and shows me some craft that she makes and from what I understand she sells these little baskets for napkins.

We try to communicate like it is all right but we both know it is not. She knows what they are like; I, on the other hand, am just learning the full story of my partner.

They are smoking crack in the kitchen. I don't believe it; I am in Portugal with a man who is meant to love me and he has left me and Jackson in the living room while he goes and smokes crack in the room next door.

I am still pissed off the next day but he just shrugs it off.

"Ah stop it! It's just a wee bit of fun. Let's go for a drive, Largo and Georgia will come (this is the couple from the previous day), we can stay at my parents' other house in Caska," he says.

We go and pick up his friends and then go for a drive with them, Jackson and their son Antonio who is six years old. As we drive through the streets I don't know where we are going. The streets are high and we are winding through the centre of Lisbon over to Rato.

"Do you want an ice cream?" they say as they both jump out the car. Then I knew it, they were away to score. I watch the people in the streets. There are lines of junkies from intermittent doors all along the sides of the house. I am scared for the safety of me and Jackson. We hear the sound of sirens and Paulo and his mate jump back into the car and we are off. They have me, Jackson, this woman and her Antonio in the car and they are scoring coke and smack.

We stop in Belem. "What are you doing?" I ask him under my breath so as not to alarm anyone else.

"Chill out, it's cool," he says as he walks away to talk with hi friend.

"Let's go to my mum and dad's other house," says Paulo.

When we arrive he tells me to put Jackson to bed and Georgia puts Antonio to sleep as well. When I come back I see he has got out the crack pipe.

"Come on, just try some," he insists, "let's enjoy some time together."

I try some, I get high and I feel like the top of my head is going to blow. It is as if the crack is trying to leap out my head and then I come down. All I can feel is a real hunger, a desire and a want, my brain is shouting, "More NOW!" The high lasts all of five minutes and then it is over and the high is not anything worth talking about.

"Why, why do you like this stuff?" I ask Paulo. "It makes you crazy and costs so much and lasts so little."

"This is fucking good shit, eh," he says, not listening to or hearing what I am saying. I go to bed and cuddle into my son and I feel alone, disappointed and scared for my future.

The next day Paulo has a plan. "We will go and take Jackson to my mum and then I will take you to this beach I know that is lovely, Costa de Caperica," he explains.

"Can't we take Jackson with us and spend some time together?" I ask.

"It is too hot and anyway my mum and dad want to spend some time with him," he says, so we go to the beach. I am sitting on the beach with him, thinking this is nice, to spend some time with him, just chillin', swimming and sunbathing.

"Let's go up to the cliffs over there for a little bit and see the view," says Paulo.

"Yeh, that would be nice." The heat on the beach is taking it out of me so it's a good idea to take a break from the beach. We drive up the cliffs and go for a walk to see the views. I am still angry about his behaviour over the previous days.

Paulo starts to get all freaky and wanting sex. I am not adverse to sex at all but I am with a man that had been treating me like shit and taking crack for the last two days. It is not a turn-on. "I don't feel like it," I tell him, which means 'how you could expect me to feel sexy when you are being such an arsehole and I am having difficulty even standing your company?' Then suddenly, out of the blue, he is pushing me against the fence that separates me from the cliff drop, saying, "Oh come on, you're my girlfriend, you are supposed to want to fuck me."

I know there is no point trying to tell him that as a woman I need respect and love and then I would be hot for him. I know he won't listen. So I look at the nice view while he is fucking me. All I can feel is this probing of my dry vagina as he is banging me against this fence. I let him do it and as he continues I am thinking he is getting left at the airport when I get home. This is shit, but nice view though. If you know anything about me by now you will know I always try to look for the good in any situation.

He pulls up his shorts and says, "Let's go back to the beach." "Oh! You have done, have you? That was really satisfying, thanks," I say sarcastically.

We are back at the beach now and I feel like just going home. "Can we go? I am missing Jackson," I tell him.

"Not just now – soon," he replies. I feel all washed out and he is driving so I just lie on my towel in the sun; he makes me feel really bad and I think to myself that I must leave this relationship. My thoughts are broken as two of Paulo's friends have just turned up. "Ola Paulo, how are you?" says one of them called Marco

"Yeh I'm good," he says.

"This is Pedro," Marco says, introducing his friend.

"This is Katie," Paulo introduces me.

"Hello," I say. I am feeling so vulnerable lying topless on the beach. It is all right when you don't know anyone but when his friends arrive I start wishing that the sand would open up and swallow me.

"I am going for a beer, do you want anything?" asks Paulo.

"Yes, can I have an ice cream please? Don't be too long, I want to go home," I tell him. "I will be back soon," reassures Paulo.

I don't know how long he has been but it seems like ages. I want to enjoy this holiday but I have had more fun when I have been on my own with Jackson.

"Hey how are you," asks Paulo. He is back looking really happy with a dozy smile on his face and a beer in his hand. "Where is my ice cream?" I ask.

"Oops sorry, I forgot," he replies nonchalantly.

"Do you think we could go now?" I ask.

"Not right now, I need some time to chill," is his response.

"Have you been on something? I have to get back to Jackson, my breast milk is oozing out my body and look at you – you are out your face and drunk and you are supposed to be driving, my son is miles away and I don't know how to get to him."

I am becoming hysterical at the lack of care and love I am feeling and also at the hopelessness of my situation.

"All right, all right, don't give me hassle, you are embarrassing me," says Paulo.

"I am going to give a lift to Marco and Pedro," he says.

"Well thanks for asking me how I feel about it." Now I look like a demented woman to his friends and I hate this, it is not who I am.

We are in the car now heading to what I hope is home to Jackson. Paulo still has a beer in his hand; this is his second as far as I know and God knows what he is on. I am scared as he is driving erratically.

"Will you stop drinking please? I happen to like my life and love Jackson and want to get to him," I plead.

"Chill out, will you," he laughs.

"Paulo, hide the beer, there is a road block," warns Marco.

"Ah don't worry, I will go this way," he says in a stupid voice like he has no fear or care. Then he starts to speak in Portuguese to the two men that are in the back seat. I feel so unsafe after his recent treatment that I don't trust him and I turn around and see these two men I don't know speaking and laughing in a language I don't know. Their faces start to contort with laughter when they see my terror. I look at Paulo and he is passing me a sly smirk and then laughing. I feel like opening the door and throwing myself on to the road in my fear but I also want to hold on and see my son again.

I am following the traffic, looking at the signs, trying to see somewhere that I recognise but I don't understand anything. I look at Paulo again. He is driving and I think this is supposed to be the man I look to for support and safety and he is a arsehole. If I get out here alive me and him are over. He casts me a sideways glance and then pulls up in a street; I have no idea where we are.

"Let's go for a beer," Paulo suggests.

"Let's get me to our son," I say and before I can say any more they are all out the car. I am frozen to the spot.

"Come on, you can't stay in there," Paulo says. "Do you want a drink?"

"I will have a coke and lemon please," I say as I find my 'used so many times' survival mode kicking in, and I know I have no choice until my feet touch down in Via Nova and my son is in my arms. We walk into this café and there are lots of men playing cards. The walls are all tiled in traditional Portuguese tiles. We leave the café after the 'men' have talked then we are back on the rollercoaster of hell, otherwise known as the car. It is getting dark now. Finally I can see Via Nova as I am starting to break at the seams. Paulo is pissed and I am hoping my angels are looking after me as I need some help. Just as we are arriving at the turn-off to the estate, Paulo looks at me and I see a glint in his eye. He turns past the estate and up the hill in order to prolong my torment and then proceeds to pull up to a café at the top of the hill. I can see Via Nova from where I am and he is having another drink.

I wait outside, exploding with fear which I can't show and anger for this bastard that I have had a child with. He comes out the café. "You all right?" he winks with a knowing smile.

"You are a dodgy bastard," I shout, "take me to my son."

"Don't you mean 'our son'?" he replies.

We get in the car and he drives to his friend's house to drop them off, then to his mother's. It is ten o'clock and I have missed Jackson all day. My breasts are sore and swollen with unused milk and I am a wreck. I cuddle into Jackson and leave Paulo to speak with his parents, probably spouting bullshit. He then goes out which means he will sleep all day tomorrow and I will have to deal with Jackson on my own, feeling the pressure of not knowing the language. I feel as if I hate his dad.

Two nights before we leave Portugal Paulo is going out again. I overhear his mother scolding him for always going out and reminding him that I have never been out any night with him. He comes into the room. "Do you want to come to this club my friends are putting on?" he asks.

"Yes, let's do it, I haven't been out to a club yet." I jump at the chance.

We go to a nightclub in the back of some place on the outskirts of Lisbon. It is in rural Portugal, sort of ghetto-like. As I enter the place I notice it is a café that has a DJ and the lights down low. The place is full of Africans, I am the only white person there. I feel cool and as always am going to enjoy myself.

"Let's have a dance," I say to Paulo.

"No, I want a drink," he responds and heads for the bar. As soon as he gets there he drops me, obviously not wanting to be with me. I see him go over and sit at a table full of women and he sinks down right in the middle of them all. He seems to know them and he doesn't even buy me a drink. I am so used to his behaviour now that I almost expect it. He does not deserve me, so I go buy myself a drink and start having a dance, which as you know is one of my passions. A good-looking young Portuguese man starts dancing with me, it is real deep African music and I love it right down to my soul.

I start to get into a good rhythm with this guy and we dance for some time. I have given up on Paulo. I refuse to ruin my only night out on my holiday with his childish behaviour. I keep looking back and see he is in oblivion again and he is driving again. I know I will have to get up with Jackson so I decide to call an end to my fun. I walk over and slide down next to him and secretly slip his car keys out of his pocket as I don't want a dead father for my son. I have now learned a lot of Portuguese after many dinners with 20 Portuguese families, dinners with my translation dictionary. I go and ask the bar man if he knows of anyone going to Via Nova in a taxi. Fortunately there is and we share a taxi and before I know it I have left Paolo to his depraved bullshit and am at home cuddling Jackson; I will take no more of his shit.

I am woken up suddenly by this breath smelling of alcohol. He is spitting with fury but with his volume control turned down low so as not to wake Jackson and his family.
"What you fucking doing, bitch, where are my car keys, what am I going to tell my dad? I had to leave the car." Paulo is home.
"Why don't you tell him you had too much to drink so you were being sensible and didn't want to drive home?" I suggest.
"Fucking smart bitch aren't you, eh?" His venom is spitting all over me and I am scared but don't show it.

He goes into the living room and starts to drink the wine from the fridge.
"Paulo, that is enough," his mother tells him. He then goes and

244

falls asleep on the sofa in the living room, with his identity card and papers and wallet lying all over the floor. I look at the mess that is my man and I look at his mother looking at him with a sad face.

"Look, he is 39 years old. I cannot do anything with him, I am sorry, I will be leaving him at the airport and that is it, I am through with him," I tell his mum.

I leave him at the airport when I get home. I am nice about it and I phone his brother to tell him that he will be alone at the airport if he wants to be there for him. His brother's reply is, "Leave him, I don't care, he made his own bed and he must lie in it."

Now this is not the end of the abuse in the relationship that I allow myself to endure. It takes me a further year to actually leave him as he keeps on creeping in on my weaknesses, and before I know it or ask for it he is living with me again. I can't tell you everything that went on between us but, as you may have gathered, this is a bad relationship. But I know I have to try everything I possibly can to save it before I gather the power to leave it.

I wear his, Jackson's and my picture around my neck to show my love. I focus on my behaviour, keeping a diary to make sure leaving him is not a mistake. It is hard to leave someone you think you love. But what is love?? Some good times and more bad? This has more bad times. If someone is squashing your person mentally or physically it is scary to leave and walk into the unknown, but you have to trust you will be all right in the end.

I have had enough of his abusive calls, him harassing me in the street and not looking after Jackson; I don't feel safe in my home anymore. I keep driving up to the Highlands with Jackson and a tent to hide from him. As I sit in the rain I wonder if I am crazy. Why is it me with the child who is forced to run? I make a decision in that tent silently before packing it and drive home.

I share my decision with Paulo.
"I have bought a ticket to Australia; do you think that is far enough?"
On that note I left for a long walk around Australia alone with Jackson. At least it is not raining!

Useful numbers

Child Line 0800 11 11

Drugs info   Frank 0800 77 66 00 / 24 hours

Alcohol Drink line 0800 917 82 82

NSPCC 0808 800 5000 / 24 Hours

Samaritans 08457 90 90 90 / 24 hours

Scottish Domestic Abuse 0800 027 1234 / 24 Hours

Napiers Homeopath 0131 225 5542

Reiki Therapist Aberdeen
Zoe Toussaint 07762902575

My websites

www.soul-pole.com

www.newhorizon.piczo.com

AUTHORS BiO

Sian Young has come a long way from her 'street days', and after seven years on the streets of Scotland she has blazed a trail in business, not letting any obstacle overcome her. She is now the head instructor and founder of Soul-POLE - an award winning business in Aberdeen. Sian has also gained many qualifications which include Meditation Teacher, Reiki Master, Pole Fitness Instructor, ETM (exercise to music) Level 2, Zumba Instructor and PADI Rescue Diver.

After coming off the streets, Sian was 6 stone and malnourished and found herself bedridden for two years at the age of 22, so being able to take part in so many sports now is real testament to how far she has come both physically and mentally. Not only did she raise her business with no initial start-up funding or business education, only the desire and determination to make it happen, she also gained two awards in her first two years of business:

The winner of 'Grampian Business Awards emerging Entrepreneur of the year 2009' and
Winner of 'Highly Commended Health Destination Clubs and Gyms Category' Trend lifestyle Awards 2010, sponsored by David Lloyd.

Sian and Soul-POLE made it onto the news again in 2011 when they hosted 'The World's Most Famous Pole Dancer' at Soul-POLE have a look at the video. http://www.youtube.com/user/danceforursoul - also showing a video of when she was just starting her business in her living room.

She is now the first Level 2 qualified pole dance instructor in the whole of Scotland, making her and her team the most highly qualified in the pole fitness industry in Scotland. There is no stopping her: she uses her determination to inspire people to help with her charity work, raising thousands of pounds a year to help build a school in Tanzania for street kids, a subject obviously close to her hear. Sian believes we all have the power to change our life; this book showing what it was really like as a young girl on the streets of Scotland; a raw, open and truly empowering account of this part of her journey.

Sian now promotes self-confidence, freedom of expression and creativity through Fun & Fitness in her Soul-POLE Classes. To find out more about Soul-POLE and all it has to offer please refer to these links:

w: www.soul-pole.com
f: http://www.facebook.com/pages/Soul-Pole-Dance-And-Fitness-Studio/142862475758929
t: http://twitter.com/#!/Sian_SoulPOLE
ln: http://uk.linkedin.com/in/soulpole

Business Member

Living is about giving. So, when you buy this book, we adopt and protect a tree for an entire year on your behalf. THANK YOU!

B1G1 moves giving from an ad-hoc, event-driven model to a very specific transaction-based giving model — a world where every transaction gives back and makes a difference.

It means that giving becomes an effortless habit, changing our lives and making a difference every second, every day and in every way.

So now B1G1 brings the power, resonance and 'connected-ness' of transaction-based giving and Impact-Based Giving to the literal hundreds of thousands of small-to-medium-scale enterprises (SMEs) that form the backbone of every economy.

Imagine if every time you dined out,
a hungry child received a meal.

Imagine if every time you bought a book,
a tree got planted.

Imagine if every time you bought an art work,
a blind person received the gift of sight.

And imagine if every time you bought or sold something, it made a difference.

Effectively, efficiently and effortlessly.
Enter the world of Buy1GIVE1,

where everything we do makes a difference.
Every second, every day and in every way.

B1G1's operations are structured to provide maximum transparency and effectiveness:

Buy1GIVE1 is a social enterprise established in 2007 (headquartered in Singapore). It supports, inspires and educates businesses globally.

B1G1 Giving is a Not-for-Profit Society registered and regulated in Singapore. It supports many other charity organisations around the world to create sustainable contribution models.
100% of contributions made by B1G1 Businesses are passed directly to the Worthy Cause organisations through B1G1 Giving. B1G1 takes nothing from the contributions nor does it receive funds from charities in any way for the services it provides.

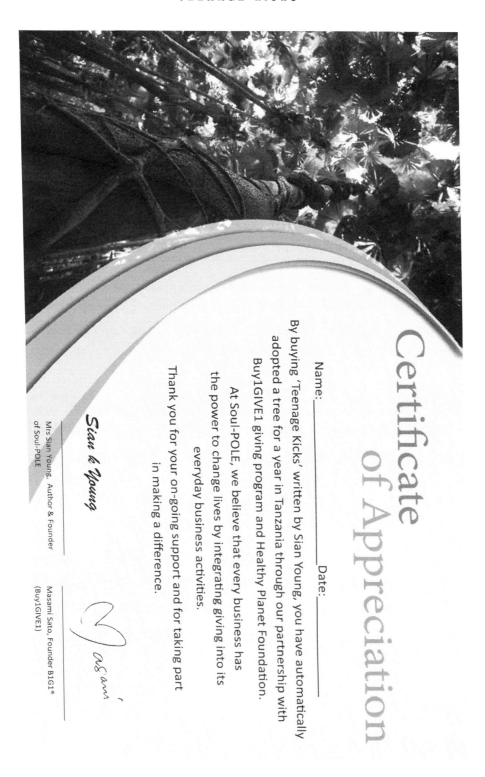

Certificate of Appreciation

Name: _____ Date: _____

By buying 'Teenage Kicks' written by Sian Young, you have automatically adopted a tree for a year in Tanzania through our partnership with Buy1GIVE1 giving program and Healthy Planet Foundation.

At Soul-POLE, we believe that every business has the power to change lives by integrating giving into its everyday business activities.

Thank you for your on-going support and for taking part in making a difference.

Sian le Young

Mrs Sian Young, Author & Founder
of Soul-POLE

Masami Sato, Founder B1G1
(Buy1GIVE1)

3643583R00141

Printed in Great Britain
by Amazon.co.uk, Ltd.,
Marston Gate.